CRITICAL DECISIONS

Literature-Based Life-Skill Lessons For Young Children

WRITTEN BY

Beth Neathamer-Mohon

ILLUSTRATED BY

Harry Norcross

BETH NEATHAMER-MOHON

Beth Neathamer-Mohon has been in the education field for 17 years. She taught lower elementary for nine years and has been a counselor for eight years. Beth enjoys writing stories, uses the stories she writes with the children in her guidance program at school, and has found the stories help make learning more fun. Beth lives in Kentucky with her husband, her daughter, Hope, and her cat and two dogs. Beth dedicates this manuscript to her husband, daughter, and extended family.

Critical Decisions: Literature-Based Life-Skill Lessons For Young Children

10-DIGIT ISBN: 1-57543-137-8
13-DIGIT ISBN: 978-1-57543-137-6

COPYRIGHT © 2006 MAR*CO PRODUCTS, INC.
Published by mar*co products, inc.
1443 Old York Road
Warminster, PA 18974
1-800-448-2197
www.marcoproducts.com

CONTENTS

Egner
5/08

Egner
5/08

INTRODUCTION

Every day children make many routine decisions. They must decide what to wear to school, what equipment to play on at recess, and even what to buy for lunch. But children must also make more serious decisions—critical ones—and need special daily guidance so they can become the best they can be.

I have heard a Native American parable in which a child told his father he felt like there were two wolves fighting in his mind—each one trying to control him. The boy told his father that an evil wolf was constantly instructing him to do bad things and a good wolf was constantly instructing him to do good things. The boy asked which wolf his father thought would win. The wise father answered, "The wolf that you feed the most will win."

In other words, whichever instructions the child chose to follow most often … good or evil … would determine which wolf would be in control.

As a school counselor, I believe it is our responsibility to help children tune in to the "good wolf" so they will decide wisely when making critical decisions in life.

The lessons in this book will help children become more knowledgeable about the critical decisions in life and the importance of making wise choices. Some of the critical decisions addressed in this book involve deciding to treat others fairly, deciding to think positively, and deciding to be drug-free. I encourage you to use this book in guiding your children to make the critical decisions that will help them become the best they can be.

Sincerely,

Beth Neathamer-Mohon

THE CRITICAL DECISION TO
BE KiND

Lesson Plan Objectives:

1. Read the story to the children for the purpose of teaching them about the importance of making the critical decision to be kind.

2. Discuss the questions before or after reading the story to encourage thinking/talking about the results of choosing to be kind or unkind.

3. Select one or more follow-up activities to give children practical experiences of kindness.

 **LESSON**

Introduction:

▸   Begin the lesson by asking:

> *If you heard something was* critical, *would you think it was* serious *or* not serious? (serious)

▸   Then say:

> *If that is true, let's play a little game. I'm going to name some things. If you believe they are critical, stand up. Another word for* important *is* critical. *If you do not believe they are critical or important, stay seated:*

> - *An operation*
> - *A bus ride*
> - *Eating dinner out*
> - *A war*
> - *Getting lost in a mall*

> *You may think some of the things I mentioned are critical and some are not. You would be sort of right, because everything can be critical at one time or another.*

          CRITICAL DECISIONS © 2006 MAR•CO PRODUCTS, INC. 1-800-448-2197

Now, what do you think the word decision *means? (Pause for student responses.) Yes, a decision is what you choose to do about something.*

If we put the two words critical decisions *together, you will know what we will be learning about. Remember when I said you were sort of right that some of the things I mentioned were not critical? That is because any of them* could *have been critical. After we hear our story about a lion that makes the critical decision to be kind, I'll tell you what I mean.*

Story:

▸ Read *Lion Learns Not To Be Rude* (pages 13-19).

▸ When you have finished reading the story, say:

I said earlier that after we read the story, I would tell you how each of the situations I mentioned when we started our lesson could be a critical or important decision. For example:

An operation—Whether to have an operation is always a critical decision. That's because it is a life-and-death matter, no matter how simple the operation seems to be.

A bus ride—A bus ride may not seem to be a critical decision, but it is if a person is not sure which bus to take to reach his or her destination.

Eating dinner out—Eating dinner out may not seem to be a critical decision, but it could be for someone who has food allergies. For that person, deciding what to eat is a critical decision.

A war—War is full of critical life-and-death decisions.

Getting lost in a mall—Being lost is a serious situation and deciding where to find help is a critical decision.

Discussion Questions:

▸ Present the following questions to the children. Remind them of the critical decision to be kind.

1. *What should you decide to do if you hear someone saying bad things about a friend of yours?* (Tell a teacher what you overheard, ask to speak with a counselor to work out this problem, nicely tell the person who was making the bad comments that you care for the person he/she is talking about, etc.)

2. *What are some kind things you could do or say to someone who has a broken leg and can't play?* (Ask the gym teacher if you may sit and talk with the person with the broken leg, write a nice note to the student with the broken leg, draw a picture showing the student that you care about him/her, etc.)

3. *What are some kind actions you could take during a day at school?* (Open the door for someone, smile at people, compliment others, etc.)

4. *Does choosing to be kind help someone to be his or her best?* (Yes.)

   How? (He/she will have more friends, get along better with people, keep out of trouble, etc.)

5. *What are some troubles people might have if they choose not to be kind?* (These people may not have friends, may not be able to get along with others, may get into trouble a lot, etc.)

Follow-Up Activities:

ACTIVITY #1

▸ This activity will show the children that being kind is important, because it helps others feel good.

▸ Materials needed: Paper and pencil for each child.

- Distribute a sheet of paper and pencil to each child. Have the children put their names on the paper and return it to the leader.

- If time allows, the leader should write a kind statement on each child's paper, then read aloud the statement written about each child. (Have each child stand as the leader reads his/her complimentary statement, then have the other children clap.)

- Distribute the sheets of paper at random, making sure that no child has his/her own paper. Direct the children to write another nice statement or draw a nice picture about the person whose name is on paper and sign their own name below their contribution.

- Collect the papers. Proofread them to make sure they contain only positive statements or pictures before returning them to their original owners.

ACTIVITY #2

- This activity requires the children to select and perform three acts of kindness in one day.

- Materials needed: Paper and pencil or crayons for each student. Chalkboard and chalk for the leader.

- The leader can model acts of kindness by saying and/or writing on the board three kind actions he/she plans to perform that day. (Example: A note mailed to a mother telling her she is loved, a call to the Post Office expressing appreciation for delivering mail even when the roads are snowy and icy, a treat that will be distributed to the students at recess.)

- Distribute paper and pencil or crayons and instruct the children to write or draw three acts of kindness they will perform that day. At the next meeting, set aside time for the children to report to the class what acts of kindness they performed and how both they and the person receiving the kindness felt.

ACTIVITY #3

▸ This activity reviews the differences between being *kind* and *unkind*.

▸ Materials needed: None

▸ Read aloud the actions listed below. Tell the children to listen to what you are saying and signal *thumbs-up* if what you are describing is an act of kindness and *thumbs-down* if it is not.

- *Opening the door for someone* (thumbs-up)
- *Whispering in front of other people* (thumbs-down)
- *Interrupting others when they are talking* (thumbs-down)
- *Sharing your crayons/supplies* (thumbs-up)
- *Raising your hand before you speak in class* (thumbs-up)
- *Cleaning up any mess you make* (thumbs-up)
- *Crowding in line* (thumbs-down)
- *Complimenting others* (thumbs-up)
- *Making fun of someone's clothes* (thumbs-down)
- *Cheating at a game* (thumbs-down)
- *Helping someone clean out his or her desk* (thumbs-up)
- *Help someone put on his or her jacket* (thumbs-up)
- *Returning something you borrowed* (thumbs-up)
- *Always trying to be first* (thumbs-down)
- *Taking turns swinging on swings on the playground* (thumbs-up)
- *Not taking turns swinging on swings* (thumbs-down)
- *Picking up litter on the playground* (thumbs-up)
- *Yelling in class* (thumbs-down)
- *Saying words like* thank you *and* please (thumbs-up)

CRITICAL DECISIONS © 2006 MAR✶CO PRODUCTS, INC. 1-800-448-2197

LION LEARNS NOT TO BE RUDE

"Hmmmm," thought Lion, who was looking for a new home. "This jungle looks like a fine place to live. Here is a great watering hole and everything looks nice and pleasant—not like that unfriendly jungle I just left. I think I will stay here."

Just then, Zebra came across Lion.

"Hi! You must be new here! I'm Zebra, and it's good to have you in our jungle," said Zebra.

Lion just looked at Zebra. He didn't answer her. Then he turned and drank from the watering hole.

"Didn't you hear me?" asked Zebra, a little louder. "Hello … nice to see you. Would you like me to show you around our jungle?"

This time, Lion *did* speak. He said, "Grrrrrrrr!!!!!" in a loud, growling voice. "I have pronounced myself king of this jungle and I will speak only to those I choose. But know this! I am better than any other animal in the land! So I will not be needing you, or any other animal, to show me around MY VERY OWN JUNGLE! I am very capable of doing this myself! Now, Zebra … I am hungry … I command you to find me something to eat and bring it to me immediately!"

Zebra ran away quickly. She was so shocked at how rude and scary this newcomer was that she told all her friends about Lion.

"Well, I *never*!" replied Monkey. "I can't believe he was so hateful and terrible. Hopefully, he will get better. Maybe he is just tired from his journey to our jungle. I'll go and see how he is acting now."

"Good luck," replied Zebra.

Monkey went to the watering hole, where he saw Lion.

"Hi Lion," said Monkey in his kindest voice. "I see you have come to our jungle. It's nice to have you here. I'm Monkey."

Lion responded with another growl. "GRRRRRRRRR!!! I can plainly see who you are, thank you. And for your information, this jungle is not OUR jungle any more. It is MY jungle. Furthermore, I clearly told Zebra that I wanted my dinner brought to me and she did not do this! I am demanding that YOU bring dinner to me, and I want it QUICKLY!"

Hearing Lion's scary tone of voice, Monkey scampered away. "Oh, my!" exclaimed Monkey to himself. He is not kind at all! Zebra is right. He is *terrible*!"

Snake, Tiger, and Hippo tried to be nice to Lion, too and they did not have any luck. Lion was just plain rude and awful!

The animals did not know what to do. But they knew they had to do something, so they got together to discuss the problem.

"I have never in my life met anyone so ugly-acting," said Snake. "He is not being kind to any of us. He thinks he is better than we are, and he is hateful to us all!"

"I wish he had never come to our jungle," agreed Tiger.

"But what are we going to do?" asked Hippo.

Just then, they heard a loud roar from the direction of the watering hole. That was where Lion was.

"Oh, my! I wonder what is going on with him now?" said Hippo.

"I don't know," said Zebra.

They heard the roar again. It sounded like Lion was in trouble.

"Rooooarrrr!"

"We should go and see what is happening," said Snake.

"I'm afraid it's a trick. He may want to eat one of us for dinner. He sure was wanting his dinner when I talked with him earlier," Zebra said in a worried tone of voice.

"I'm afraid of that, too," admitted Monkey.

"Well, let's just sneak over there and look at what is going on," said Tiger. "I'll protect all of you from him."

The other animals reluctantly agreed. They followed quietly and closely behind Tiger to see what was going on with Lion.

When they got to the watering hole, they were surprised.

"Help, Help, HELP!" shouted Lion.

"Oh, my!" cried Zebra. "He has slipped into the quicksand and he is sinking. He refused to let me show him around our jungle, so he didn't know about the quicksand!"

The animals looked at each other, wondering what to do. Then Snake spoke up. "We can't just let him sink," he said. "We have to help."

The other animals hesitated. They weren't sure they really wanted to do anything.

Reader: Pause. Ask the children the following questions, then continue reading the story.

Is this a critical decision? (Yes.)

Why? (Because the situation is serious. It is a matter of life and death.)

The animals knew they had to make a critical decision and they had to make it fast. There was no way they could leave Lion in the quicksand, so they agreed to help him … and just in time.

Snake wrapped himself around a strong tree and the others clung to each other. They formed a chain until Zebra was close enough to reach Lion in the quicksand.

"Grab on!" shouted Zebra just before Lion's head started to sink. Lion grabbed onto Zebra and Zebra and the others started pulling.

"Pull hard!" shouted Monkey.

The animals pulled and pulled and pulled. Finally … Lion, with the help of all the animals pulling with all their strength, rose slowly, but surely, out of the quicksand.

After he was safe, Lion looked around at all the animals that had saved his life. He stared at each animal silently. No one said a word.

Finally, after a very long time, Lion took a long, deep breath and spoke. "Friends," he said, "I have learned a great lesson today."

Lion sighed and took another long, deep breath before he spoke again.

"I have always considered myself to be better than all other animals. I have been very unkind. I know now that I shouldn't have been so hateful. You could have left me in the quicksand, but you rescued me. I am truly grateful."

Lion paused before he spoke again.

"I left my other jungle because no one was kind to me and now, for the first time, I understand why they weren't. I wasn't kind to them!"

Lion's eyes showed his regret. He even seemed to be trying to hold back tears as he continued.

"I want to say that I am sorry and ask all of you for another chance. I am making a critical decision this very moment to be KIND to others from now on."

Reader: Pause. Ask the children the following questions, then continue reading the story.

Why is deciding to be kind a critical decision for Lion? (The situation is serious.)

Why? (If Lion did not change his behavior, he would not be liked by the other animals, just as he had not been liked in the jungle where he had lived before.)

"I know now," continued Lion, "that being kind will help me to be my best. I will change from being rude to being kind. Please forgive me. I am truly thankful to all of you for saving my life. I am also grateful that you taught me this valuable lesson. I know now how important it is to be kind."

"You are welcome, Lion," Zebra responded. "I think I speak for all the animals in saying that we are glad you learned this lesson about the importance of being kind and we are also glad that we were able to save you. In our jungle, we do our best to treat each other with kindness. As long as you agree to be kind and not growl at us all the time, I think we will all get along very well."

"Yes," echoed all the other animals in unison.

Lion smiled a big smile, showing all his bright teeth … and … then … the animals heard another big growling sound coming from Lion. "Grrrrrrrr."

"You weren't serious! It was a trick!" They all screamed and huddled together in a tight circle.

Lion looked confused, then laughed. "Oh, my, friends! Don't worry about that growling sound! That is just my stomach growling. I am hungry and would sure like to eat some … berries! Would you mind showing me around OUR jungle so I can learn where berries grow?"

The animals all laughed with Lion when they realized he was not going to hurt them. They all visited, laughed, and chatted as they walked to the berry patch to pick berries for their dinner.

The jungle was a happy place again because everyone had made the critical decision to be kind.

THE CRITICAL DECISION TO THINK POSITIVELY

Lesson Plan Objectives:

1.   Read the story to the children for the purpose of teaching them about the importance of making the critical decision to think in a positive manner.

2.   Discuss the questions before or after reading the story to encourage thinking/talking about the results of choosing to think in a positive manner.

3.   Select one or more follow-up activities to give children practical experiences in positive thinking.

 **LESSON**

Introduction:

▸   Begin the lesson by asking:

   What does it mean to decide to think in a positive manner? (It means instead of focusing on what is bad, to think about what is good.)

   Can someone turn something bad into something good just by deciding to think in a positive manner? (Yes.)

▸   Then say:

   We are going to play a little game to prove that we can turn something bad into something good just by deciding to think in a positive manner. If I say something that is an example of positive thinking, wave your hands in the air but do not touch anyone else. If I say something that is not an example of positive thinking, keep your hands still.

   A person decides to think the following:

   •   *It is awful when it rains!* (Not positive. Keep hands still.)

- *I'm glad it is raining so we can be cozy inside and watch movies.* (Positive thinking. Wave hands.)
- *I am sad that I failed my spelling test!* (Keep hands still.)
- *I know I will do better on the next spelling test because I will study harder.* (Wave hands.)
- *I am upset because my best friend moved away.* (Keep hands still.)
- *I am glad that I have a computer so I can e-mail my friend who has moved.* (Wave hands.)
- *I feel upset because I didn't win the game and my friend did.* (Keep hands still.)
- *I am glad I have a friend to play games with.* (Wave hands.)
- *I hate that I broke my arm.* (Keep hands still.)
- *I am glad I didn't break the arm I write with.* (Wave hands.)

▶ Continue the lesson by saying:

You have just made several decisions about positive thinking. A critical decision is a decision that is serious. Is the decision to think positively a critical decision? (Yes.)

Why? (A person who thinks about or sees only the bad effects of a situation will feel miserable. But a person who looks for the good in a situation will have a better attitude and be happier.)

▶ Introduce the story by saying:

Today we are going to hear a story about a little frog that makes the critical decision to use positive thinking to try to turn a bad situation into a happy one.

Story:

▶ Read *Little Rosie Frog's Rose-Colored Glasses* (pages 25-30).

▶ When you have finished reading the story, ask:

Can you see how a bad situation can be turned around to be happy, or at least not as bad, if you make the critical decision to think positively? (Yes.)

Discussion Questions:

▶ Present the following questions to the children. Remind them of the importance of the critical decision to think positively.

1. *How can positive thinking turn this situation from bad to better? You have to go to the doctor because you are sick.* (You can decide to be happy that you have a doctor who can help you feel better.)

2. *How can positive thinking turn this situation from bad to better? You have homework to do after school today.* (You can decide to be happy that you will be smarter after you complete your homework.)

3. *How can positive thinking turn this situation from bad to better? You are sad because you twisted your ankle.* (You could be glad that you didn't break your leg.)

Follow-Up Activities:

ACTIVITY #1

▶ This activity allows the children to review ways of identifying positive and negative thinking.

▶ Materials needed: Red transparency strips cut to fit so the children can hold them over their eyes and look through them.

▶ Discuss that *positive thinking* means the same thing as the phrase "Trying to see the world through rose-colored glasses."

▸ Distribute a red transparency strip to each child. Tell the children to hold the strips to their eyes in order to see the world through rose-colored glasses.

▸ Repeat the introductory activity. This time, instead of waving hands or keeping them still, have the children hold the red transparency strips to their eyes when you describe an example of positive thinking and keep the transparency strips on their laps when you describe something that is *not* an example of positive thinking.

ACTIVITY #2

▸ This activity allows the children to practice using positive thinking to change a bad situation into a better one.

▸ Materials needed: The following sentences written on strips of paper. Do not write the words in parentheses. These words are the answers.

1. I am mad because I have to go to the dentist today. (Deciding to think positively—I'm glad I have a dentist so my teeth will stay healthy and pretty.)

2. I hate what we are having for lunch today. (Deciding to think positively—I am glad I have food to eat.)

3. I am sad that I didn't make the goal in our soccer game. (Deciding to think positively—I will do better next time.)

4. My friend has been mad at me all week. (Deciding to think positively—I am glad I have a teacher/counselor who will help my friend and me work out our problem.)

5. I have only one pet and I want another one. (Deciding to think positively—I am glad that I have at least one pet.)

▸ Divide the class into five groups. Give each group of children one of the sentence strips and have them discuss how positive thinking can change the negative statement into something better. You may have to read the sentence strips out loud to younger children. Set a time limit for the activity and have the children share their conclusions.

ACTIVITY #3

▶ This activity will encourage children to use positive thinking to change a bad real-life situation into a better one.

▶ Materials needed: Red transparency strip for each child. Cut the red transparencies into strips the right size for the children to hold up to their eyes and look through.

▶ Distribute a red transparency strip to each child. Then say:

> *Many things will happen throughout the day. If something happens that you do not like, decide to think about it in a positive manner and write or draw how the situation could be viewed in a more positive way. For example: If it is raining outside, you could look through the red transparency strip and think, "It is raining now. If it is okay with my parents, I can have fun jumping in the puddles when I get home."*
>
> *Keep your red transparency strip with you to remind you to see the world more in a more rosy way."*

▶ At the next meeting, have the children describe their "rosy" decisions to the class.

CRITICAL DECISIONS © 2006 MAR*CO PRODUCTS, INC. 1-800-448-2197

LITTLE ROSIE FROG'S ROSE-COLORED GLASSES

Little Rosie is a little frog that lives in a small creek beside a nice clear, green pond. Little Rosie woke up one morning and peered out of her frog hole. She noticed a dark cloud passing by. "Oh, rats!" exclaimed Little Rosie. "It's going to rain today. I don't want it to rain today. Mama! Can you make the clouds go away?"

Mama Frog wisely answered, "My, you certainly got up on the wrong side of the bed this morning. That's not a good way to greet the day. No, I can't make the clouds go away. But I do know a trick to help you *kind of* make the clouds go away."

"Tell me. Tell me," insisted Little Rosie Frog.

"Well, come over here," said Mama Frog, "and hop into my lap." Little Rosie Frog hopped right into Mama Frog's lap. "The trick, Rosie, has a lot to do with your name."

"My name?" asked Little Rosie Frog.

"Yes," answered Mama Frog. "I want you and I to try a trick to see the world like it's a bit more bright and rosy, just like your name."

"How?" asked Little Rosie Frog.

"Here," said Mama. "Pretend to put on some rose-tinted glasses, and I will do the same."

Mama Frog pretended to pull a pair of glasses from her pocket and put them on. She then pretended to hand another pair to Little Rosie Frog. Little Rosie Frog smiled as she pretended to put on her glasses, too.

"Now let's look outside. And this time, let's see if we can see anything that looks a bit more rosy," said Mama Frog.

"OK," said Little Rosie Frog.

Mama Frog and Little Rosie Frog looked out of their burrow and began to talk.

 CRITICAL DECISIONS © 2006 MAR∗CO PRODUCTS, INC. 1-800-448-2197

"It does look like it is going to rain. I see some dark clouds," said Mama Frog.

"Yep, it does look like it is going to rain. My friend Butterfly can't play with me in the rain. She has to hide under something until the rain stops," said Little Rosie Frog.

"That's true," said Mama Frog.

"Fishy gets to play with me in the rain," Little Rosie Frog said quietly.

"Hummmm," said Mama Frog. "That last thing you said sounded a bit rosy to me."

"What?" asked Little Rosie Frog.

"Instead of deciding to keep saying what is bad, you found something to say that is happy," said Mama Frog. "You said that you and Fishy can still play together in the rain."

Reader: Pause. Ask the children the following questions, then continue reading the story.

Is the decision to use positive thinking a critical decision? (Yes.)

Why? (If you focus on what is bad all the time, you won't be happy.)

"Now that I think about it, Fishy and I have had a lot of fun in the rain. Why, one rainy day, we raced across the pond and blew bubbles in the water," Little Rosie Frog said gleefully.

"It sounds like you both decided to have a rosy, happy day because you both decided to think positively," said Mama.

"We sure did. Maybe we can do it again today," said Little Rosie Frog.

"You sure can, Little Rosie Frog, as soon as you get some breakfast," said Mama Frog.

"OK," said Little Rosie Frog. "I want fly pastries."

"I'm sorry, honey. We have run out of fly pastries. I'll get more at the store later."

"No pastries! I want pastries!" complained Little Rosie Frog.

"Rosie, do you still have on your pretend rose-colored glasses? I still have mine on," said Mama Frog. "Maybe they can help us decide to think in a more positive way."

Mama Frog pretended to adjust her glasses. Then she pretended to adjust Little Rosie Frog's glasses. Then Little Rosie Frog and her mother began to talk again.

"We're out of pastries," said Mama Frog.

"I know," said Little Rosie Frog, "and my mouth is watering for fly pastries."

"I know," replied Mama Frog.

"Hey, Mama!" shouted Little Rosie Frog, pretending to adjust her rose-colored glasses. "I remember one time I helped you make bug muffins for breakfast. You let me stir the batter."

"Hummmm … I remember that. We had fun, didn't we? It was a rosy morning!" said Mama Frog.

"It sure was! You let me lick the bowl, too," Little Rosie Frog said excitedly. "Do we have what we need to make bug muffins?"

 CRITICAL DECISIONS © 2006 MAR✳CO PRODUCTS, INC. 1-800-448-2197

"We sure do," said Mama Frog as she opened a kitchen cabinet. "Here is a mix for bug muffins right here! Rosie, how did you turn from being upset to being happy?" she asked.

"I just decided, with my rose-colored glasses, to be happy about not having pastries, because now we can make muffins!" Little Rosie Frog said gleefully.

Reader: Pause. Ask the children the following questions, then continue reading the story.

Is Little Rosie Frog learning how to think in a more positive way? (Yes.)

How can you tell? (She didn't let not having pastries upset her for very long. She decided to think positively, and this helped her find a solution to her problem and be happy again.)

After that statement, Mama Frog and Rosie laughed. This was positively rosy! Then they stirred, and *this* was positively rosy. Then they giggled and licked the bowl. This was positively rosy, too. A little while later, they were able to eat the muffins. And this was positively rosy for sure!

Then Little Rosie Frog went outside and played in the rain with Fishy. They giggled, splashed, and raced across the pond. Little Rosie Frog won that race! Playing with her friend and winning the race was positively rosy!

Then Little Rosie Frog and Fishy competed to see who could blow the biggest bubble. (Fishy won this contest!) And Little Rosie Frog did not think that was rosy AT ALL!

"You cheated," said Little Rosie Frog.

"I did not," responded Fishy. "I don't want to play with you any more," said Little Rosie Frog, and she started to hop home. But then she remembered her pretend rose-colored glasses, stopped, and thought for a bit.

"Hmmmmmm … I think I can decide to think positively about this situation. I'm happy that I won the race across the pond. Maybe I should be happy that Fishy won something, too." Little Rosie Frog pretended to put on her rose-colored glasses and didn't waste another second.

Little Rosie Frog yelled out to her friend, "Fishy I'm sorry for being hateful." Little Rosie Frog had decided to be positive so she and Fishy could still have fun. She even told Fishy that he had blown the biggest bubble that she had ever seen. That made Fishy feel good and made Rosie feel especially rosy!

Fishy and Little Rosie Frog played the rest of the day together and had lots of fun.

When Little Rosie Frog got home, she hopped up into her mother's lap. She told her mother how she remembered about her rose-colored glasses and how she had decided to think positively with Fishy.

Little Rosie's mother hugged her tightly and said, "Rosie, your rose-colored glasses will always remind you to make the critical decision to think in a positive way. I think my Little Rosie Frog is going to have many rosy days ahead."

Both Mama Frog and Little Rosie Frog adjusted their pretend rose-colored glasses and smiled big rosy smiles.

THE CRITICAL DECISION TO
HELP OTHERS

Lesson Plan Objectives:

1. Read the story to the children for the purpose of teaching them about the importance of making the critical decision to help others.

2. Discuss the questions before or after reading the story to encourage thinking/talking about the results of choosing to help others.

3. Select one or more follow-up activities to give children practical experiences in helping others.

 LESSON

Introduction:

▸ Begin the lesson by teaching the children the following song to the tune of *"Mary Had A Little Lamb."*

>H-el-ping is good to do.
>Good to do.
>Good to do.
>H-el-ping is good to do.
>It shows that you're a friend.
>
>H-el-ping is good to do.
>Good to do.
>Good to do.
>H-el-ping is good to do.
>Friendships will never end.

▸ Ask the children:

>*Why do you think helping is a good thing to do?* (Helping is good to do because it shows others that you care about them and that you are a good friend to them.)

Why do you think helping might be fun? (Helping others can be fun because it makes you feel happy.)

How can helping cause you to have more friends? (Helping others lets people know that you are a good person and would be a good friend. Therefore, helping others can result in friendships.)

Story:

▶ Introduce the story by saying:

A critical decision *is when you must make a serious decision about something that is happening to you or someone else. Today you are going to hear a story about a character that makes the critical decision to help others. If you listen closely, you will also learn how making this critical decision can help you.*

▶ Read *Patty Possum's Pouchful Of Love* (pages 35-43).

Discussion Questions:

▶ Present the following questions to the children. Remind them of the importance of making the critical decision to help others.

1. *What are some ways you can help others at school?* (a. If someone in your class is sick, you could give this person a card or call, so he/she will know that you care. b. If someone at your school is lonely, you could help this person feel better by talking with him/her. c. You can help your teacher by listening to what he/she is saying. This will help your teacher teach more and will help you to learn more.)

2. *What are some ways you could help your family?* (a. You can help your family by doing chores around the house, such as cleaning your room or doing the dishes. b. You can help your family by being respectful to your parent or guardian. c. You can help your family by being polite to your sisters or brothers.)

   CRITICAL DECISIONS © 2006 MAR✶CO PRODUCTS, INC. 1-800-448-2197

3. *What are some ways you could help your community?* (a. You can help your community by not littering. b. You can help your community by volunteering in a place that helps others such as a resthome, daycare center, or church. c. You can help your community by obeying rules and laws.)

4. *If you do not help others, what could happen?* (If you do not help others, you will not have very many friends. There may come a time when you need help and, if you have not helped others, they might not help you.)

5. *If you help others, what will probably happen?* (If you help others, they will know that you are a caring person and would be a good friend to have. When you need help, others will help you because you helped them.)

Follow-Up Activities:

ACTIVITY #1

▶ This activity will give the children practice in helping and experience in making future critical decisions about helping others.

▶ Materials needed: None

▶ Ask the principal what deeds your students could do to help your school. Then perform some of these acts as a group. For example:

- Pick up trash on playground.
- Plant flowers or trees in the schoolyard.

ACTIVITY #2

▶ This activity will help the children experience the good feelings resulting from making a critical decision to help others.

▶ Materials needed: None

▸ Assign each child a secret pal. Each secret pal can help his/her assigned partner have a good day. Some suggestions on how to help a secret pal have a nice day are:

- Draw a picture and leave it on his/her desk.
- Leave a nice note on his/her desk.
- Put a treat, such as a piece of candy or a new pencil, on his/her desk.

ACTIVITY #3

▸ This activity will help the children set goals to act on their critical decision to be kind.

▸ Materials needed: Paper and pencil and/or crayons for each child.

▸ Distribute the paper and pencils and/or crayons to each child. Have the children assign themselves *Help Homework.* Each child should write down or draw three things he/she will do that would help someone at home. After the children have had time to complete their homework assignment, allow time for each child to share what he/she has written. Then say:

> *Take your papers home and check off each item on your list after you have completed it. Then turn your homework in to me.*

▸ You may want to write on each homework page how proud you are of the child's helpful deeds.

(Note: This could make a good bulletin board display. Hang up the homework papers and label the bulletin board: *I Am A Helper.*)

PATTY POSSUM'S POUCHFUL OF LOVE

"Mama, what are all the things you have used your pouch for?" asked Patty Possum.

Mama Possum smiled and said, "Oh, my little Patty, a pouch is such a wonderful thing to have! When I was little, I used my pouch for many fun things. I would sometimes carry my baby dolls around to practice being a mama. I would sometimes put my paws in my pouch to keep them warm. I would sometimes take walks and pick up pretty things to show my mama when I got home. I would see how full I could stuff my pouch.

"When I was grown, of course, I used my pouch to carry you. Now I use my pouch to help my family. I carry snacks and toys for you and I carry my grocery list to make sure I buy the right foods to make good suppers for us. You are very lucky to have a pouch, sweetie.

"What are you thinking you want to do with your pouch?" asked Mama Possum.

"I sure like your idea of collecting things!" Patty Possum said excitedly as she raced around her mama. "I want to get my pouch as full as can be!"

"Well, it is a beautiful day," said Mama Possum, smiling. "Why don't you walk in the meadow near our house and collect a pouchful of special things? I'll be here making our lunch, so when you come back we can eat while you show me what you have collected. I am looking forward to seeing all the things you bring back. This will be a fun lunch, I'm sure."

"Yes, it *will* be a fun lunch!" said Patty Possum. "I will have lots of stuff to show you when I get back."

"Well, have fun, sweetie," said Mama Possum. "I'll call you when lunch is ready. Be sure and come right away so your lunch will be hot. I'm making soup and sandwiches."

"OK, Mama, I will. See you in a bit," said Patty as she ran off into the meadow. Patty was very eager to find special things to show her mother.

"Wow!" said Patty as she came to a stream. "I never really paid any attention to how many pretty things there are here. I see lots of pretty things already!"

Patty moved closer to the stream.

"Look at these pebbles!" she exclaimed to herself. "They look so smooth and shiny!"

Patty saw a bunch of pretty pebbles. There were three that really sparkled.

"I'll put the three prettiest ones in my pouch to show Mama," she said happily.

Then Patty continued on her way.

"Oh! I see more neat things. Acorns! Goodness, there are a lot of them. They really look neat. They remind me of someone wearing a hat," laughed Patty. "I'll put a bunch of these in my pouch, too. Mama will like looking at these!"

Patty Possum gathered up a lot of acorns, then went on her way.

"Oh! I see some beautiful leaves," Patty said as she hopped over to a colorful tree. "I can put a bunch of these bright leaves in my pouch, too."

Patty collected some of the prettiest leaves that were on the ground under the tree.

"Wow! My pouch is already getting full of special things. Mama will be proud of me!" Patty said excitedly.

Just then, Patty Possum saw Little Bunny sitting on a tree stump close by. Patty thought her friend looked sad.

"What is wrong, Little Bunny?" Patty asked.

"I'm not feeling well today," said Little Bunny. "My stomach hurts from eating too many carrots this morning for breakfast. Ohhhhhh … it really hurts."

Patty felt sorry for Little Bunny and began to think, "Mama uses her pouch to carry things to help our family. Maybe I could use my pouch to help, too. I could use my pouch to help my friend. After I help, I can collect more things for Mama to see."

Then Patty told Little Bunny, "Here, Little Bunny. I found some really pretty rocks by the stream today. You may have them. Maybe they will help you stop thinking about not feeling good and start to help you to feel better."

Little Bunny took the three pretty rocks. "They are beautiful," said Little Bunny admiring at how they sparkled in the sunlight. "You are a good friend. I think they are already helping me feel better. Thank you."

"You are welcome," said Patty as she went happily on her way.

Reader: Pause. Ask the children the following questions, then continue reading the story.

When Patty decided to help her friend, was that a critical decision? (Yes.)

Why? (It was a critical decision because friends help each other. When Patty made the critical decision to help Little Bunny, Little Bunny knew that she really cared for him. If she did not help, her friend's stomach might have hurt longer.)

A little later, Patty spotted another friend and went over to see her.

"Hi, Greta Groundhog," said Patty Possum. "What are you doing?"

"Shhhh," whispered Greta Groundhog. "I am baby-sitting my little nephew. I just got him to go to sleep."

Patty saw the tiny groundhog that Greta was holding.

"He is precious," said Patty Possum.

"He sure is," Greta agreed proudly. "The only thing is … I just got him to sleep and now I'm very hungry. I can't get something to eat because if I get up, I am afraid that I will wake him. GGGGRRRR … Hear my stomach growling?" asked Greta.

"I sure do," Patty said softly.

Reader: Pause. Ask the children the following questions, then continue reading the story.

If Patty decides to help Greta Groundhog, will that be a critical decision? (Yes.)

Why? (Greta Groundhog needs help and Patty is her friend. Friends should help friends, if they can. If she did not help, both Greta and her nephew would have problems.)

Patty thought again. "Here is another chance to help someone, just like my mom helps me."

Then Patty whispered to Greta, "I have been collecting some neat things from the meadow and I just collected a lot of leaves. They are really pretty, so maybe they will taste good to you. Here, you may have them to eat."

"Oh, thank you so much, Patty! I'm starting to feel like I'm about to starve," said Greta, smiling at the pretty leaves.

Greta Groundhog munched the leaves and her nephew groundhog slept right through the meal.

"Mmmmmm, that *was* tasty! Thank you very much," Greta said again.

"Glad to help," said Patty Possum as she went on her way again.

Patty thought to herself, "My deciding to help others makes *me* feel good, too."

Patty soon ran into her friend, Little Deer. He looked nervous and like he was in a hurry.

"What's wrong, Little Deer?" asked Patty.

"Oh my! I am in such a hurry and everything seems to be going wrong," her friend said. "I am supposed to be having a surprise birthday dinner for my neighbor, Mr. Squirrel. I thought I had everything ready, then I dropped my glass bowl with all the acorns I had collected for him onto the floor. I had to throw them away because they were dirty and had glass on them. What am I going to do?" cried Little Deer. "Mr. Squirrel and his family are to be at my house in just a few minutes, and I don't have time to fill my basket with acorns again and clean up the mess in my kitchen before they all get here."

Reader: Pause. Ask the children the following questions, then continue reading the story.

Do you think Patty will again make the critical decision to help her friend? (Yes.)

What do you think she will do? (She will probably give Little Deer the acorns she collected.)

What might happen if Patty did not make the critical decision to help Little Deer? (If she did not help Little Deer, he would continue to be upset and Patty might feel guilty. Their friendship might suffer.)

Patty smiled. "Don't worry, Little Deer. I have been collecting things today and I have a lot of acorns in my pouch. You may have them for your surprise dinner."

Patty reached into her pouch, took out all the acorns, and quickly filled Little Deer's basket.

"Oh, my! Oh, my … I don't know what to say! Thank you so much. I am so grateful to you for this!" Little Deer exclaimed.

"No problem! I am glad to help," Patty said happily.

Just at that moment, Patty Possum heard her mother calling for her.

Then Patty remembered, "I was supposed to have a bunch of pretty things in my pouch to show Mama while we ate lunch. I don't have anything and now I don't have time to get anything either."

Patty was a little upset as she made her way home.

Reader: Pause. Ask the children the following questions, then continue reading the story.

Why do you think Patty was upset? (She was upset because she told her mother she would bring back things for them to look at during lunch and she does not have anything to show her mother. Her pouch is empty because she gave away the things she had collected in order to help her friends.)

Do you think Patty's mother will be upset that Patty did not bring back things for them to look at? (No.)

Why? (After Patty's mother hears all the helpful things she decided to do for her friends, she will be proud that Patty made the critical decision to help others.)

"Hi, sweetie," said Mama Possum. "Put your special treasures on the table and we'll talk while we eat."

Patty looked sad and Mama Possum could tell something was wrong.

"What is troubling you?" asked Mama Possum.

"Well," Patty explained, "I found a lot of things. But then I thought of how you used your pouch to help us, so I decided to be like you and use my pouch to help my friends."

"What do you mean?" asked Mama Possum.

"I had some pretty rocks, but I gave them to Little Bunny because he was sick. I had some pretty leaves, but I gave them to Greta Groundhog because she was hungry. And I had some acorns, but I gave them to Little Deer for Mr. Squirrel's surprise dinner. That's why my pouch is not

CRITICAL DECISIONS © 2006 MAR·CO PRODUCTS, INC. 1-800-448-2197 full of anything special any more. I thought I'd have time to collect things for us to look at, but then you called for me. That's why my pouch is empty," Patty answered sadly.

"Hmmm … " said Mama Possum smiling sweetly at her daughter. Mama Possum was quiet for a bit. Then she said, "Patty, I think you are wrong about your pouch being empty. I believe your pouch is full of something very special. Let me take a peek."

Mama Possum peeked into Patty's pouch and cried, "Why, Patty, your pouch is full all the way to the top!"

"What?" Patty was confused. "I don't see anything in there."

"Patty, your pouch is full of something you can't see with your eyes. But I can see it with my heart. Why, Patty, your pouch is FULL of LOVE."

Patty could tell that her mom was proud of her. This made her feel very happy.

"What you did today was loving and helpful," said Mama Possum. "I am more proud of you for giving your treasures away to those that needed them, than I would have been for you to keep the special things you found just to show me. You are a very helpful possum and I am proud that you are full of so much love." Mama Possum gave Patty a big hug.

Patty smiled an even bigger smile and hugged her Mama back tightly.

"Now, Patty, sit down at the table before our lunch gets cold. I'm looking forward to hearing all about your helpful adventure. This will be a fun lunch to remember for sure!"

As Patty sat down to eat, she felt very happy and proud. "I am glad I decided to use my pouch to help others," thought Patty. "This way, I'll always have a pouch that's full. It will be full of love!"

THE CRITICAL DECISION TO
BE FAIR

Lesson Plan Objectives:

1.   Read the story to the children for the purpose of teaching them about the importance of making the critical decision to be fair.

2.   Discuss the questions before or after reading the story to encourage thinking/talking about the results of choosing to be fair.

3.   Select one or more follow-up activities to give children practical experiences in being fair.

 **LESSON**

Introduction:

▸   Begin the lesson by saying:

> *If you hear me saying something that is fair, clap. If you hear me saying something that is unfair, say, "Boooo!"*

▸   Read the following statements aloud to the children:

1.   *You are playing a game of checkers with your friend. When your friend is not looking, you take some of his checkers off the board.* (Boooo!)

2.   *You and your friend take turns playing a video game that you both like to play.* (clap)

3.   *You borrowed money from a friend and you will pay her back as soon as you can.* (clap)

4.   *You quit playing a game when you realize that you are not going to win.* (Boooo!)

5. *You look at someone else's paper during a test in order to copy an answer.* (Boooo!)

Story:

▶ Introduce the story by saying:

You make a lot of decisions each day. Some are more serious than others. A critical decision is a serious decision. Today you are going to hear a story about a giraffe that makes the critical decision to be fair. After hearing this story, you will know more about the critical decision to be fair.

▶ Read *Giraffe Decides To Be Fair* (pages 52-56).

Discussion Questions:

▶ Present the following questions to the children. Remind them of the importance of the critical decision to be fair.

1. *What are some things you would do to show that you are playing a game fairly?* (While playing, you should take turns and follow the rules of the game.)

2. *What are some things that are not fair to do while playing a game?* (It would not be fair to cheat at the game. It would not be fair if you always insisted on being the first player.)

3. *What are some things you would do to show that you are being fair in a race at recess?* (If you are in a race, it would be fair to wait until it was time to start running. If you wanted to pass someone while running, it would be fair to do so without touching that person.)

4. *What are some things that are not fair to do in a race?* (It would not be fair to trip or push someone who is ahead of you. It would not be fair to start running before the other racers.)

5.   *What might happen if you chose not to play a game fairly?* (If you did not play a game fairly, people could get mad at you and not want to play with you.)

6.   *What might happen if you decided to play fairly when you played games with others?* (If you decided to play games fairly, you would probably be invited to play more games with other people.)

Follow-Up Activities:

ACTIVITY #1

▸   This activity will give the children practice in playing fairly.

▸   Materials needed: Chalkboard and chalk or marker board and markers for the leader. Copy of *Memory Game* (pages 50-51) and scissors for each group of children.

▸   Tell the children that they will play a game called *Memory* if they can help you think of rules for playing this game fairly. Write the rules on the board as they are being discussed, so the children can see the game rules that they have agreed upon. For example:

Memory Game Rules

1.   Turn the matching cards face-down. Mix them up so players do not know where the match for each card is.
2.   Have players take turns turning two cards over to see if they match.
3.   Continue doing this until each card is matched with its mate.
4.   Each player then counts the number of matches that he/she has.
5.   The player with the most matches wins the game.

▸   After agreeing on the rules and writing the rules on the board, divide the class into groups of 2-4 children.

▸   Distribute a copy of *Memory Game* and scissors to each group of children. Direct one student in each group to cut along the lines so that the 16 shapes will be in separated into 16 cards for the children to use to play the matching game. (Younger children may need you to cut for them.)

▶ After the paper is cut into 16 cards, the children will follow fairly the rules agreed upon while playing the *Memory Game.*

▶ After each group has played the game, discuss what each group did that was fair. (Groups could respond that they took turns, followed rules, and did not cheat.)

▶ Discuss why it is better to play games fairly. (It is better to play fairly because then everyone has a chance to win and there will not be as many arguments.)

ACTIVITY #2

▶ This activity will give the children a chance to see the possible consequences of cheating and the possible rewards of playing fairly.

▶ Materials needed: None

▶ Have the children role-play what someone might say or do if someone else cheated at a game.

- They might role-play telling the teacher on the cheating child.
- They might role-play saying they do not want to play with the cheating child.
- They might role-play being angry with the cheating child.

▶ Have the children role-play what someone might say to another person who played a game fairly.

- They might role-play saying, "I really enjoyed playing with you."
- They might role-play inviting the person to play another game.
- They might role-play saying, "You are a good friend because you are fun to play with."

▶ Have the children role-play how someone might feel if he/she won a game by cheating.

- They could role-play feeling guilty by hanging their heads and looking sad.

▸ Have the children role-play how someone might feel if he/she won the game fairly.

- They could role-play being happy by smiling.
- They could role-play being happy about winning, but considerate of the player(s) who did not win.
- They could say, "Good game! Thanks for letting me play. You will probably win the next time," to the player(s) who did not win.

ACTIVITY #3A

▸ This activity allows the children to see fair play modeled on a game day.

▸ Materials needed: Five or more children's games for multiple players. You will also need a container and a slip of paper with each child's name.

▸ Put the slips of paper on which children's names are written in the container. Assign which game each student will be playing by drawing the children's names from the container.

▸ After playing, the children could discuss ways they played the games fairly. (They could state that they took turns, were considerate of others, did not cheat, followed the rules, etc.)

ACTIVITY #3B

▸ This activity allows the children to observe fair play.

▸ Materials needed: One children's game that can be played by a group, container, and slips of paper with children's names.

▸ The leader should explain how to play the game, then draw 2-4 names from the container. The children whose names are drawn should come to the front of the room and demonstrate how to play the game. (Note: Conducting this activity on several different meetings gives each child a chance to be in the group that models fair play.)

▸ The children watching the game should observe the players and raise their hands when they notice any player doing something that is fair. When called upon, that child can explain how the game players were demonstrating fair play.

MEMORY GAME

GIRAFFE DECIDES TO BE FAIR

"Good morning, Giraffe," said Zebra. "Are you going to play in the jungle park today? All our friends will be there."

"Why, of course," replied Giraffe. "I'm heading that way right now. Rabbit, Hippo, Possum, and Tiger are coming, too. I talked with them yesterday."

"Great!" said Zebra. "Let's get going!"

Zebra and Giraffe met their other friends at the park. They all gave each other *high fives* and started talking about what games they were going to play.

Giraffe stated, "It's my turn to pick out the game, because I haven't gotten to do this yet. Zebra, you picked hide-and-seek and jump rope the other day, and Rabbit and Tiger, you both picked *Simon Says* and *Mother, May I?* Possum picked a chase and Hippo picked playing with the water hose. I think it would be fair if I got to pick the games for today. I have a lot of fun games in mind to play. I have been thinking of them for a long time and have them written down on this paper. See?" said Giraffe, excitedly holding out his game list.

"Wow!" said Zebra as she glanced at the list. "You *have* been thinking a lot about this. It's fine by me to let you pick. What do the rest of you say?"

"Fine with us," the animals all replied. "That would be the fair thing to do."

"Great!" said Giraffe. "I'll get started with my list. First, I want to play *Who Can Reach The Highest?* I'll start. I can reach to the top of the sliding board. How high can all of you reach?" asked Giraffe.

The other animals looked at each other in disbelief.

CRITICAL DECISIONS © 2006 MAR✳CO PRODUCTS, INC. 1-800-448-2197

Zebra finally replied, "I don't think we can beat you on that one, Giraffe. I think you won that game."

"Yeah! I won!" shouted Giraffe, jumping up and down. "Yeah for me!" said Giraffe, trying to keep from smiling. "Now let's go on to the next game. OK, the number two game is *Who Is The Tallest?* Everyone line up next to me to see who the winner of this game will be."

The animals rolled their eyes at each other, but slowly lined up as Giraffe had requested.

"Yeah! I won this game, too!" shouted Giraffe as he looked behind himself to see his shorter friends. "I won again!" he yelled.

"Isn't this fun?" asked Giraffe. "I can think of good games, can't I?"

The animals again looked at each other. Finally, Rabbit spoke up: "Let me see your list of games."

Reader: Pause. Ask the children the following questions, then continue reading the story.

Do you think Giraffe is being fair? (No.)

Why? (He is not being fair because he is playing only games that he can win.)

Giraffe proudly handed the list to Rabbit, who started to read it aloud.

"Hmmmm," she said as she began reading the list to the friends. "Let's see here. The next game to play is *Who Can Jump And Touch The Top Of The Swing Set*. The game after that is *Who Can See The Furthest Distance From The Park*, and the next game is *Who Has The Longest Neck …* "

"Giraffe!" shouted all the animals. "Your games are not FAIR!"

Reader: Pause. Ask the children the following questions, then continue reading the story.

Giraffe must decide whether to be fair. Do you think this is a critical decision? (Yes.)

Why? (It is critical because his decision will determine whether the others will like him and enjoy playing games with him.)

"Well!" said Giraffe in a very hurt voice. "I think my games are wonderful! I am having lots of fun today playing my games."

Hippo cleared his throat and spoke up, trying to use a kind tone. "Giraffe, your games are wonderful games to play with your giraffe friends and family because you are all about the same size. These games, however, are not fair to us because we are not as tall as you are. For example, let's predict who would win all the rest of the games that you listed: *Who Can Jump And Touch The Top Of The Swing Set?*"

Giraffe cried, "I can! I can! I think I would win this game!"

"Right," Hippo said very calmly, "and who would win the other games of who can see farthest and who has the longest neck?"

"I would! I would!" shouted Giraffe. "I think I would win those games, too."

"That's right," said Tiger, who was a bit grouchy. "We wouldn't have a chance to win any of those games. That is NOT FAIR!"

"Yes," said Possum, tired of not being understood by Giraffe. "Do you remember when you told us it was your turn to pick the games because we all had already had our turns?"

"Yes," said Giraffe, "I remember."

"Well," explained Possum, "just like it is not fair for you to never have the chance to pick the games, it is unfair for us not to ever have a chance to win the games you pick. You should try to play fair games where each of us has a chance to win."

"Hmmmm … ," thought Giraffe. "I never really thought about my games not being fair. I was just trying to think of fun games and I guess I was thinking that these games were fun because … " Giraffe paused and thought some more. "I think I thought they were all fun because I would win them all," he admitted.

It was then that Rabbit spoke up, "Winning is not everything, Giraffe. It is fun just to play with your friends no matter who wins, but it isn't fair to play games no one has a chance to win but you. That is not fun or fair for the rest of us. In order for all of us to have fun together, it would be nice if you make the critical decision to be fair."

"I hadn't thought of it this way, friends." said Giraffe. "You are right I *will* make the critical decision to be fair. I am so sorry about the games I had picked."

Reader: Pause. Ask the children the following question, then continue reading the story.

What must Giraffe do next to show he is truly sorry for not picking fair games? (He must pick a game that all the animals will enjoy.)

"That's OK, Giraffe," said Rabbit. "I think you have made a good decision to be fair. Since it is still your day to pick games, can you think of a fair game for all of us to play?"

"I think I can," said Giraffe. "Hmmmmm … Let's see… Oh! I know one! I've got one!" shouted Giraffe. *Ring Around The Rosie!* I love playing this game!"

"Great idea!" said Tiger. "That is a fun game that no one really wins. It is just fun to play! I like this idea!"

All the animals joined hands and circled around, playing *Ring Around The Rosie*. They laughed and played nicely with each other the rest of the day because Giraffe continued to pick games and activities that were fair and fun for everyone.

CRITICAL DECISIONS © 2006 MAR✳CO PRODUCTS, INC. 1-800-448-2197

THE CRITICAL DECISION TO
NOT GIVE UP

Lesson Plan Objectives:

1. Read the story to the children for the purpose of teaching them about the importance of making the critical decision to not give up.

2. Discuss the questions before or after reading the story to encourage thinking/talking about the results of choosing to not give up.

3. Select one or more follow-up activities to give children practical experiences in deciding to not give up.

 LESSON

Introduction:

▸ Materials needed: Sealed bag of candy and scissors for the leader.

▸ Introduce the lesson by pretending to have a hard time opening a bag of candy. Then say:

> *This is my favorite kind of candy, but I am having trouble opening the bag. I may just give up.*

> *If I do give up, what would I be missing out on?* (Children could respond: You would be missing out on getting to eat your favorite kind of candy.)

> *Yes, you are correct. If I gave up, I would be missing out on eating my favorite candy and I really want to eat this candy. I think I should decide to not give up.*

▸ Pretend to struggle some more, then try another way to open the bag by getting scissors and cutting it open. Then say:

> *I'm glad I decided to not give up. It is smart to decide to not give up, even when you have difficulties or troubles reaching your goal.*

▸ Share the candy in the bag with the children.

Story:

▸ Introduce the story by saying:

> *In today's story, an acorn must make a critical decision. The word* critical *means* serious *so a critical decision is a serious decision. Today you are going to hear a story about an acorn that makes a critical decision to not give up. If you listen carefully, the story will help you to decide to not give up, too.*

▸ Read *Sammy Seed* (pages 62-69).

Discussion Questions:

▸ Present the following questions to the children. Remind them of the importance of the critical decision to not give up.

1. *What helps you get rid of the feeling of wanting to give up?* (a. I get help from someone. b. I talk with someone who will encourage me. c. I take a break, then start again. d. I can talk to myself and remind myself to not give up.)

2. *If you have trouble reaching a goal, should you give up?* (No.) *Why?* (You will not reach your goal if you let difficulties and troubles stop you from trying.)

3. *Do you think struggles can make you stronger or even wiser, if you don't give up?* (Yes.) *Give some examples of why this could be so.* (a. If you have trouble doing your homework and you decide to ask for help, you will reach your goal and you will be stronger and wiser

because you did not give up. b. If you have trouble running a mile with your track team and you decide to keep training until you can run the mile, you will be stronger and wiser when you reach your goal because you did not give up. c. If you have trouble learning to skate and you decide to continue to practice until you know how to skate, you will be stronger and wiser when you reach your goal because you did not give up.)

Follow–Up Activities:

ACTIVITY #1

▸ This activity will give the children practice in not giving up and will help them develop their ability to help each other to not give up.

▸ Materials needed: Somewhat difficult puzzle for each student group.

▸ Divide the class into groups. Give each group a puzzle.

▸ Discuss what problems they may have as they try to work the puzzle. (They may not be able to fit the pieces in, may not get along with people in the group, may not find the pieces they need, etc.)

▸ Tell the children:

In spite of any troubles you may have, keep encouraging each other to decide to not give up until the puzzle is completed.

▸ Allow the children time to work on the puzzle. Then allow time to compliment the children for not giving up even though problems may have occurred.

▸ Ask the children how they felt when they finally reached their goal of working on the puzzle. (Proud, happy, excited, etc.)

ACTIVITY #2

▶ This activity will give the children more practice in not giving up and in helping each other not to give up.

▶ Materials needed: Large number of blocks for each group of children.

▶ Divide the class into groups and give each group a large number of blocks. Then say:

> *You are to stack the blocks as high as you can without letting them fall.* (Note: You may want to play with the blocks before you begin this activity to determine how many blocks can be stacked without falling. This will help you decide how many blocks to give each group.)

▶ Discuss the problems the children may have when trying to stack the blocks. (The blocks could keep falling, someone might accidentally shake the table, the children could get frustrated while trying to reach this goal, etc.)

▶ After this discussion, tell the children that in spite of troubles they may have, they should keep encouraging each other to not give up until the blocks are stacked.

▶ Allow the children to work with the blocks until they can stack them without any falling.

▶ Compliment the children for not giving up even though they may have had problems.

▶ Ask the children how they felt when they reached the goal of stacking the blocks. (Proud, happy, excited, etc.)

ACTIVITY #3

▶ This activity will show the children that they have reached many goals because they made the critical decision to not give up.

▶ Materials needed: Paper, pencil, and crayons or markers for each student.

▶ Have the children describe things they have accomplished in spite of difficulties or problems because they decided to not give up.

▶ Distribute paper, pencils, and crayons or markers to the children. Ask the children to write down and/or illustrate something they accomplished because they decided to not give up. Some examples of things the children could write and/or illustrate are:

- I learned to skate because I decided to not give up.
- I learned to ride a bike because I decided to not give up.
- I learned to swim because I decided to not give up.
- I learned to read because I decided to not give up.
- I learned to do math problems because I decided to not give up.

These pictures could be used to create a bulletin board.

 # SAMMY SEED

Sammy Seed was an acorn who lived high up in the sky, on one of his mama's oak branches. Sammy and his mama lived on the top of a beautiful big hill.

One day, Sammy Seed said, "Mama, I can't wait until I'm old enough for the wind to blow me off your branch. Then I can roll down our hill and find a home of my own."

"It won't be long, Sammy," said his mama. "You are growing every day. Now remember what I told you. When the wind does blow enough to make you drop and roll to your new home, don't ever give up! Settle in, start some roots, and find water. You will grow to be a beautiful, strong oak tree like me. I am proud of you, son."

"Don't worry, Mama," Sammy said. "I'll remember what you told me."

That night, Sammy Seed dreamed of rolling down the hill to a nice piece of land. In his dream, he rolled past the beautiful cool stream that ran at the base of the hill. He dreamed of snuggling into the soft soil and beginning to grow.

"I'll be so happy in my new wonderful home! I can hardly wait!" exclaimed Sammy Seed when he woke up.

Not many days after that, a strong wind began to blow.

"Sammy Seed," said his mama, "I'm excited for you! I think today may be your day!"

"I'm excited, too!" said Sammy Seed as he remembered his beautiful dream.

The wind began to pick up even more. Sammy Seed knew that his happy adventure could begin any minute.

Then the wind picked up more and even more! This was no ordinary wind. It was extremely strong! It was a … tornado! This wind was not only strong enough to knock Sammy Seed loose from his mama's branches, it was strong enough to pick him up and carry him high into the sky. The wind jostled and tossed him around. Sammy went in circles—around and around and around!

Sammy Seed was able to catch just a quick glimpse of the ground below. He saw plush land just like he had dreamed of. He could even see a river.

"Oh, boy! Oh, boy!" shouted Sammy Seed. "This is great! I'm ready to land, Wind. I'm ready to land!"

But the wind just whirled and whipped Sammy around some more, carrying him farther and farther away. Then the wind suddenly rushed downward! Sammy Seed caught another quick glimpse of the land below.

"Oh, my!" exclaimed Sammy Seed as he looked down. "This ground that I'm seeing now is not nice land at all. It is all rocky and dry. I sure don't want to land here. Wind, Wind, please don't drop me here."

But the wind did drop Sammy Seed there. And it practically shoved him down onto one of the rockiest places he could have imagined.

BOOM! BANG! BOOMITY BOOM! Sammy Seed landed hard on the stony ground.

"Oh, my shell! It's cracked now! Ouch! That hurts!" Sammy cried. "Ouch! Oh! Ugh! Ow!"

Then Sammy Seed started to roll. TUMBLE, ROLL, CRASH!

Finally, Sammy Seed stopped, with a thud, between two huge rocks.

"This is a horrible place! This is not at all like my beautiful dream. This is a nightmare! I hurt all over, and I am not happy. What am I going to do? My shell is broken and I feel as if my heart is broken, too. I am at a loss as to what to do now!"

Sammy Seed started to cry and give up. But then he remembered what his mama had told him: "When you land, don't ever give up. Settle in, start some roots, and find water."

"OK," said Sammy Seed, pretending to answer his mama, "I will do these things."

Sammy Seed told himself, "I am making a critical decision right now to not give up. I will keep trying in spite of my problems and troubles! I will find a way to settle in. I will become a beautiful tree like my mama. I will. I will. I will."

"Now, just let me get adjusted here. I can get pretty comfortable," he said as he leaned against one of the bigger rocks.

Sammy Seed made himself as comfortable as he could. "Now I need to start some roots. I am not giving up! Why, come to think of it, it may be good that my shell got broken. I can start poking out my roots sooner than if my shell hadn't been broken."

"OK," said Sammy Seed, "I'm not giving up. I'm settling in and starting roots. Next, I will find a water source."

After a few rains and a few weeks, Sammy Seed had grown upward. His roots had grown, and grown, and grown, but then another problem surfaced. Sammy still had not found a water source under the ground.

"Oh, what shall I do?" cried Sammy Seed. His roots twisted around rocks and boulders under the ground in search of water. His roots were strong and long, but Sammy Seed knew that to grow big and beautiful like his mama, he had to find water somewhere under the ground.

Day after day he searched and stretched. One day, Sammy Seed did strike water.

"Yes!" shouted Sammy Seed. "Yes! I *did* find water."

Sammy Seed finally felt content as he began using his roots like straws to drink from the underground stream. He tasted the cool, wet water. It was wonderful.

"Now I have finally done all that my mama told me to do. I did not give up. I sure felt like it when my dream of landing in a nice area did not come true. I settled in, even though it was between two hard rocks. I started roots quickly, since my shell had broken open. And now I have found drinking water! I am glad I decided to listen to my mama and not give up," Sammy Seed sighed happily.

Reader: Pause. Ask the children the following question, then continue reading the story.

Why was it a critical decision for Sammy Seed to decide to not give up?
(If he gave up, then he would not reach his goal of becoming a beautiful, strong oak tree like his mother.)

Sammy Seed felt pride swelling inside him, but once again, trouble happened.

Sammy heard a BOOM! BANG! sound again, but this time it wasn't him landing. A terrible, huge storm was approaching.

"Oh, my! What should I do?" wondered Sammy Seed.

Sammy Seed held on between the rocks and gripped his roots as tightly as he could. The rain beat down hard around him. There was so much rain, the area began to flood. The current was growing more and more fierce!

"Hold on! Remember your critical decision to not give up!" Sammy Seed coached himself.

CRITICAL DECISIONS © 2006 MAR•CO PRODUCTS, INC. 1-800-448-2197

He leaned into the rocks around him and thought to himself, "I think I'm lucky to have landed between these rocks. They are helping me hold my ground." He began to realize that his struggle to find water had made his roots very strong—maybe even strong enough to withstand this awful storm.

Throughout the night, Sammy Seed held his ground. Sammy survived the storm!

The next day, Sammy Seed felt himself grow. He grew upward with his trunk and downward with his roots, and he felt himself grow wiser.

Sammy Seed began to think more positively about his troubled start. He even thought, "I bet lots of trees would have given up when they had to struggle so much for water, but because I didn't give up, I have become stronger. I bet lots of trees that didn't have to struggle and become strong like my mother and me were possibly blown over in the storm last night."

Sammy Seed began to realize that his troubles might have been good fortunes. He had become strong and wise because he decided not to give up and decided to work through his problems.

As Sammy Seed was thinking about his experiences, he heard a small cry.

"Help, help! Last night the wind carried me to a terrible place, and my shell is broken."

Sammy Seed saw who was speaking. It was a tiny acorn blown there during the storm. He began to tell his new neighbor what his mama had taught him when he was a little acorn.

What do you think Sammy Seed is going to tell the acorn? (He will tell the little acorn to make the critical decision to not give up even though he may have problems and any problems he does have could help him become stronger and wiser.)

"Little Acorn," Sammy Seed began, "I, too, thought I was unlucky to have landed here. My shell was also broken, but this tragedy helped me to start roots earlier than I had planned to.

"I thought I was unlucky to have landed between these big rocks. But last night, the rocks kept me from being washed away by the rain.

"I thought I was unlucky to have to search so deep in the ground for water, but the search made my roots strong enough to hold on through the terrible storm.

"Little Acorn, if you decide to not give up and to work through your problems like I did, you will become stronger and better than you ever dreamed you could be. You have landed in a troubled place. But if you don't give up, working through your troubles can help you become strong and wise so you can accomplish great things."

The little acorn listened to Sammy Seed and a big smile began to light up his face.

Reader: Pause. Ask the children the following question, then continue reading the story.

Why do you think the little acorn smiled? (He smiled because he thought he would be like Sammy Seed and make the critical decision to not give up.)

Sammy Seed looked down and realized that he truly *was* becoming a big and beautiful oak tree, just like his mama.

"I am so glad I made the critical decision to not give up," said Sammy Seed. "I am so proud that I worked through my problems and became the best I could be. I have learned that there are advantages to having problems. If you decide not to give up, your problems will make you stronger and wiser than before. People may label me just another nut that held his ground, but I know I'm special. I know my mama is proud of me and I am very proud of me, too. I am proud because I did not give up!"

THE CRITICAL DECISION TO
MAKE GOOD CHOICES

Lesson Plan Objectives:

1. Read the story to the children for the purpose of teaching them that the decision to make good choices is a critical life-skill.

2. Discuss the questions before or after reading the story to encourage thinking/talking about the results of making good choices.

3. Select one or more follow-up activities to give the children practical experiences in making good choices.

 **LESSON**

Introduction:

▶ Begin the lesson by presenting the following introductory activity:

- Draw an imaginary line down the middle of the classroom.
- Tell the children that one side of the room represents *good* choices.
- Tell the children that the other side of the room represents *bad* choices.
- Tell the children that the middle of the room (imaginary line) represents being *undecided* as to whether the decision is good or bad.

▶ Have the children stand on the imaginary line in the middle of the room. Then say:

I am going to give you some choices. When I say, "Move," you should move from where you are to the side of the room that represents how you feel about the choice. If you have no opinion or are not sure whether the choice is good or bad, you may remain where you are.

Begin the activity by saying:

You have an important test tomorrow and you decide to watch TV instead of studying. Move. (Children should go to the side of the room that represents a bad choice.)

Then ask:

Why is this a bad choice? (It is a bad choice because you probably will not do well on the test if you spend your time watching TV instead of studying.)

What would be a good choice in this situation? (It would be a good choice to study for the test on this night and plan to watch TV another night.)

Have the children move back to the center of the room, then continue the activity by saying:

Your grandmother comes over for dinner. After you say hello to her, you go to your room to play video games. Move. (Children should go to the side of the room that represents a bad choice.)

Then ask:

Why is this a bad choice? (This is a bad choice because you are missing a chance to visit with your grandmother and your actions could hurt her feelings.)

What would be a good choice in this situation? (It would be a good choice to spend time with your grandmother while she is at your house. This would show good manners and be a good time for you to get to know your grandmother better. You can play the video games after she leaves.)

Have the children move back to the center of the room, then continue the activity by saying:

Your parents ask you to be quiet because your little brother is sleeping. After hearing your parents' request, you turn down your radio and close your bedroom door to keep your brother from waking. Move. (Children should go to the side of the room that represents a good choice.)

Then ask:

Why is this a good choice? (It is a good choice because if you are quiet, your brother will not wake up and you will not be in trouble with your parents.)

Have the children move back to the center of the room, then continue the activity by saying:

Your mother gives you a list of chores to do before you can go out to play. Instead of doing what is on the list, you sneak outside to play with your friends. Move. (Children should go to the side of the room that represents a bad choice.)

Then ask:

Why is this a bad choice? (It is a bad choice because it is disrespectful to your mother and you probably will be in a lot of trouble.)

What would be a good choice in this situation? (It would be a good choice to do your chores, then ask if you may to go outside to play.)

Have the children move back to the center of the room. Present the last situation by saying:

Someone offers you a piece of candy and you take it. Move. (Children should stay in the middle of the room that represents being undecided about whether this is a good or bad choice.)

Then ask:

Why are you undecided about this choice? (You would have to have more information about the person who offered you the candy. If you knew the person, it would be OK to accept the candy. If you did not know the person, it would be a bad choice to accept the candy because you would not know if the candy is safe to eat.)

Story:

▶ Introduce the story by saying:

> A critical situation *is a* serious situation. *The situations we just talked about were critical situations. If you had made a poor choice about any of them, it would be a serious mistake. It is always important to make good choices. In the story we are going to hear, we will meet a hippopotamus that learned making good choices were critical decisions.*

▶ Read *Little Hippo Learns About Choices* (pages 78-84).

Discussion Questions:

▶ Before asking the discussion questions, explain the following strategy that helps people make good decisions.

D.I.G.S. Strategy

D: DETERMINE what the problem is.
I: IDENTIFY some options/choices you can use to solve the problem.
G: GO with the best option/decision to solve the problem.
S: SEE if this option/decision worked. If it did not, START the strategy over again. SEEK help this time if you need it.

▶ Present the following questions to the children. Remind them of the importance of the critical decision to make good choices.

1. *What are some things that can help you make a good choice when you are confused about what to decide?* (You can think through the situation by using the *D.I.G.S. Strategy*.)

2. *Who are some people who can help you make good choices when you do not know what to decide?* (A teacher, counselor, parent, relative, neighbor, or friend may help you make good choices.)

▶   Present the following scenario to the children. Say:

> *Your best friend sees that the girl who sits next to you in class is absent and has left money in her desk. Your best friend suggests that the two of you steal the money.*

Instruct the children to use the *D.I.G.S. Strategy* to determine the best way to resolve the problem. (Note: You may need to guide younger children through the process.)

D: DETERMINE what the problem is. (Your friend has suggested that the two of you steal your classmate's money.)

I: IDENTIFY some options/choices you could use to solve the problem. (a. I could steal the money with my friend and our classmate would probably never find out who took it. But I would feel really guilty even if I did not get caught. If I *did* get caught, my classmate would not trust me and I would be in a lot of trouble. b. I could tell my friend I would not feel right stealing the money, then I could change the subject and talk about something else.)

G: GO with the best choice to solve the problem. (I will decide to go with "b" because it is the best way to solve the problem and keep out of trouble.)

S: SEE if the children chose an option/choice that would work. If they did not, START the strategy over and help them think of people from whom they could SEEK help.

Follow-Up Activities:

ACTIVITY #1

▶   This activity will give the children practice in using the *D.I.G.S. Strategy*. With your guidance, they will learn the steps involved in the critical decision of making good choices.

▶   Materials needed: Paper, pen, container, bucket of sand, newspapers, and toy shovel for the leader.

▶ Write the following statements on strips of paper.

   1. You find some money on the playground as the bell is ringing to go inside.
   2. Your classmate asks to copy your spelling test.
   3. You broke your friend's video game.

Place the strips of paper in a bucket filled with sand. Put the bucket of sand on some newspapers to minimize the mess.

▶ Write each child's name on a piece of paper and place it in the container.

▶ Draw a child's name from the container. Hand this child the toy shovel. (The shovel will help the child remember the *D.I.G.S. Strategy*.) Ask the child to "dig" carefully in the bucket to find a strip of paper.

▶ When the child finds a strip of paper, have him/her read it aloud. Ask the children to discuss with each other a good decision using the *D.I.G.S. Strategy*. (Note: You may need to read the sentence strips to younger children.) Call on a few children to tell the class what they talked about and decided. If necessary, help the children review the *D.I.G.S.* steps for each sentence strip.

Scenario #1:

You find some money on the playground as the bell is ringing to go inside.

   D: DETERMINE what the problem is. (What should I do with the money I found on the playground?)

   I: IDENTIFY some options/choices you could use to solve the problem. (a. I could keep the money and not tell anyone that I found it. But if I kept the money, I would feel guilty. If I got caught, I would be in a lot of trouble. b. I could give the money to the teacher who could find out who lost it.)

   G: GO with the best choice to solve the problem. (I will pick "b" and give the money to the teacher so he/she can find out whose it is. I won't feel guilty, and my teacher will be proud of me.)

S: SEE if the children chose an option/choice that would work. If they did not, START the strategy over and help them think of people from whom they could SEEK help.

Scenario #2:

Your classmate asks to copy your spelling test.

D: DETERMINE what the problem is. (My classmate wants to copy my spelling test.)

I: IDENTIFY some options/choices you could use to solve the problem. (a. I could choose to let him/her copy my work, but I would feel guilty about this choice. If I got caught, we would both be in trouble. b. I could ignore this classmate during the test and later say that I will help him/her study for the next test.)

G: GO with the best choice to solve the problem. (I will choose "b." I will ignore my classmate and later say that I will help him/her study for the next test. I will not get into trouble and I will be helping my friend, too.)

S: SEE if the children chose an option/choice that would work. If they did not, START the strategy over and help them think of people from whom they could SEEK help.

Scenario #3:

You broke your friend's video game.

D: DETERMINE what the problem is. (I broke my friend's video game and I must make a choice about what to do next.)

I: IDENTIFY some options/choices you could use to solve the problem. (a. I could put the game on my friend's desk when he/she is not looking. When my friend asks me about it being broken, I could say that it was working when I put it on the desk and someone else must have played with it and broken it. But if I choose to do this, I would feel guilty. If my friend ever found out that I was lying, he/she would not trust me anymore. b. I could tell my friend the truth and say that I will use my allowance to pay for a new game.)

G: GO with the best choice to solve the problem. (I will choose to tell the truth and pay for the broken video game. My friend will trust me and I will not have to feel guilty.)

S: SEE if the children chose an option/choice that would work. If they did not, START the strategy over and help them think of people from whom they could SEEK help.

ACTIVITY #2

▸ This activity will give the children practice making good choices in real-life situations. It is called *Good Choices Homework.*

▸ Materials needed: None

▸ Instruct the children to remember one or two good choices that they make between now and the next meeting.

▸ Inform the children that, at the next meeting, you will be calling on volunteers to describe good choices they decided to make.

LITTLE HIPPO LEARNS ABOUT CHOICES

"Little Hippo, I have your chore list for the day here on the kitchen table. Be sure and do these chores before you go outside. I have a big day planned for all of us," said Mama Hippo, "and I want you to finish your chores as soon as you can.

"Do you remember the little talk your dad and I had with you about your being old enough now to decide to make good choices? Well, I want you to decide to do what is right. For several weeks now, you have chosen not to do your chores," complained Mama Hippo, "and your father and I are about talked out."

"I know, Mama. I listened to your talks," Little Hippo grumbled as he picked up the list and his mother went into the other room. "Hmmmm, let's see here … OK, I can do this. The list doesn't look too bad today. I am to fill the birdbath with fresh water. I am to make my bed and straighten my room. Lastly, I am to put my bike away in the shed. I left it outside yesterday."

Little Hippo put the list down and looked out the window. It was Saturday morning and it was a beautiful day. The birds were singing and the sun was shining. He stared out the window some more and thought, "This would be a great day to play with my friends at the watering hole."

With the beautiful day in mind, Little Hippo thought, "I think I will call my friends and play with them first, then do my chores later. This is what I am going to choose to do. Mama said she had a big day planned for us. I bet her big plan is for us all to clean out the garage. I heard her say the other day that it needed cleaning up. I sure don't want to do that. It doesn't sound like any fun."

CRITICAL DECISIONS © 2006 MAR*CO PRODUCTS, INC. 1-800-448-2197

With that thought, Little Hippo called his friends to see if they could go swimming. All of them asked their parents and were allowed to go with him to the watering hole! Little Hippo was excited.

Reader: Pause. Ask the children the following questions, then continue reading the story.

Was Little Hippo making a good critical decision at this time? (No.)

How do you know? (Little Hippo decided to go to the watering hole with his friends instead of doing his chores. This will get him into more trouble with his parents.)

Little Hippo knew he should do his chores first, but he was not making good choices today. He even chose to sneak out the side door of their house before his mother could catch him. Off he ran to meet his friends.

Later, when Mama Hippo had finished her chores for the day, she called for Little Hippo. "Little Hippo, have you finished your chores yet? You are going to be excited when you find out what I have planned for all of us to do together today."

Mama Hippo waited and waited. She did not hear Little Hippo coming.

"Hmmmm," thought Mama Hippo when she noticed that Little Hippo was not around. Then she noticed that none of his chores had been done. "Hmmmm," said Mama Hippo again. "I bet I know where he is."

Mama Hippo followed the path to the place Little Hippo had gone. She hid behind some large bushes and, sure enough, saw Little Hippo and his friends playing together in the watering hole.

Reader: Pause. Ask the children the following questions, then continue reading the story.

How do you think Mama Hippo felt when she saw Little Hippo at the watering hole? (She probably felt disappointed in Little Hippo.)

Do you think Little Hippo is going to be in trouble? (Yes.)

Why? (He will be in trouble because he did not decide to do what was right. It was a critical decision and he made the wrong choice.)

"OK," thought Mama Hippo, "I am through talking with Little Hippo about making critical decisions and good choices. I think today will be a good day to teach Little Hippo a lesson about the importance of making good choices."

Mama Hippo called Little Hippo's grandmama and explained everything. His grandmother agreed and said she would be right over. Then Mama Hippo called for Baby Hippo and Daddy Hippo.

"Is everyone finished with their chores and ready to go to the county fair? Mama Hippo asked. "Baby Hippo and I have just now finished our jobs around the house," answered Daddy Hippo.

"All of us except Little Hippo have finished our chores and are ready to go to the fair," said Mama Hippo. Then she explained what had happened.

"Hmmmm," said Daddy Hippo. "I certainly agree it is high time our little son learned about making good choices. I think the only way he is going to learn to do that is to experience the consequences for making bad choices."

About that time, Grandmama Hippo arrived and said she would be glad to hippo-sit Little Hippo while Mama, Daddy, and Little Hippo went to the fair.

"Thank you," Mama and Daddy Hippo said to Grandmama Hippo. "We appreciate your help. It is a shame Little Hippo can't go with us, but he has to start making good choices."

Mama, Daddy, and Baby Hippo went on to the fair. Grandmama Hippo waited in the house for Little Hippo to come home.

Later that afternoon, Little Hippo came home. His grandmama waved to him when he came in the door.

"Where are Mama and Daddy? Where is Baby?" asked Little Hippo.

"Oh, your mom and dad went to the fair today after they finished their chores," his grandmama said. "They took Baby Hippo with them. That was the big day your mother was speaking of this morning. You weren't here and you had decided again not to do your chores. They asked me to watch you while they were gone."

Little Hippo cried. Then he got mad! "AGGGH!" shouted Little Hippo. "They should have taken me, too."

"Well," said Grandmama, "did you decide to do your chores, like your mother asked you to or did you decide to sneak down to the watering hole?"

Little Hippo had to admit that he hadn't made good choices today. He started thinking about the critical decisions he had faced recently and the poor choices he had made. He had been making poor choices for quite a while. This made him sad and angry. Not angry with his parents, but angry with himself.

"Grandmama, I am sorry for how I have been acting. What should I do?" Little Hippo asked sincerely.

"We all have to learn hard lessons sometimes," his grandmama said. "I think you are learning that it pays to think through your choices and try to always make the best ones. Since you chose to not do your chores, it wouldn't be fair to allow you to go to the fair. But it's never too late to start making good choices. Why don't you make the critical decision today to start making better choices?"

Little Hippo smiled and agreed. "I am going to make better choices from now on. This is my critical decision."

"Now," said Grandmama Hippo, "let's take a look at your chore list. Hmmmm … I see several lists here that your Mama and Daddy left."

Little Hippo looked at the lists his grandmother was holding. "Oh, these are the lists from today and from several days back. I haven't been doing my chores for a while now."

"Well," said Grandmama Hippo, "there's no time like the present to get started. I'll help you mark them off as you finish them. I'll bet you can finish a lot of these chores before they come home. I'll also bet that this will make your parents very proud of you."

"I want them to be proud of me," said Little Hippo. "I really have learned a lesson."

Little Hippo worked very hard the rest of the afternoon and into the early part of the evening, doing all the chores he had been putting off. When he was finished, he felt better and even proud of himself.

Grandmama Hippo was very proud of Little Hippo, too.

Reader: Pause. Ask the children the following questions, then continue reading the story.

Do you think Little Hippo has learned that it is a critical decision to make better choices? (Yes.)

How can you tell? (He has started making better choices by doing his chores and he seems to be sorry for the way he had been acting. He has learned that not making good choices can lead to a lot of trouble.)

When his grandmama asked him to show her what he had done, Little Hippo showed her how neat and clean his room was. His closet, too. He showed her that his bike was put away and that there was fresh water in the birdbath. He also showed her that the porch was swept and his toy shelves were organized. He even was able to show her that the weeds had been pulled from the flower beds and that his tree house was clean.

Grandmama Hippo complimented Little Hippo on what a great job he had done. She was pleased. Little Hippo started being glad that he was making good choices. It felt good to do what was right.

When Mama, Daddy, and Baby Hippo came home, Little Hippo said, "I am so sorry for not making good choices. I have learned a good lesson today. I know now that it would not have been fair for me to go to the fair. I really am sorry. I think that next year when the fair comes, I will deserve to go."

Mama and Daddy Hippo looked around at all the good work Little Hippo had done and they each gave him a big hug. They hugged Grandmama Hippo, too. They were very proud and happy.

"We are so proud of you, son," said Daddy Hippo. "I don't think you will ever have to miss the fair again. What's fair is fair, and I'm fairly sure you have learned to make good choices. Good for you, son."

Reader: Conclude the story by asking the children the following question:

Using the D.I.G.S. Strategy, what could Little Hippo have decided when his mother told him to do his chores?

D: DETERMINE what the problem is. (Little Hippo was supposed to do his chores, but he did not want to do them.)

I: IDENTIFY options/choices that Little Hippo had. (a. Little Hippo could have continued to not do his chores, but this would cause him to continue to get into trouble with his parents. b. Little Hippo could have decided to do his chores first and play later.)

G: GO with the best option/choice to solve the problem. (Little Hippo should have decided to do his chores first and play later because that choice would have kept him out of trouble.)

S: SEE if this option/choice would work. (Yes, it would work.)

THE CRITICAL DECISION TO KEEP PROMISES

Lesson Plan Objectives:

1. Read the story to the children for the purpose of teaching them that keeping their promises is a critical life-skill decision.

2. Discuss the questions before or after reading the story to encourage thinking/talking about the results of choosing to keep your promises.

3. Select one or more follow-up activities to give children practical experiences in keeping their promises.

 ❂❂❂❂ **LESSON** ❂❂❂❂

Introduction:

▸   Materials needed: Piece of unlined paper and crayon for each child.

▸   Introduce the lesson by asking the children:

   What is the meaning of the word promise? (A *promise* is a pledge that you will do what you say you will do.)

   Should people keep their promises? (Yes, people should keep their promises.)

▸   Distribute a piece of paper and a crayon to each child. On the front of the paper, tell the children to draw a big smiley face. On the back of the paper, tell the children to draw a big frowning face.

▸   Then say:

   I am going to read some statements aloud. After I have read them, hold up either the frowning face or the smiley face to show how you feel about what I have read.

(Note: The leader may want to demonstrate how to keep a promise by holding a similar piece of paper up after the statement is read and the children have made their decisions.)

▶ Read the following statements aloud:

1. *I promise to pass out candy to everyone at the end of the day. How does this make you feel?* (Children will hold up the smiley face.)

2. *Pretend that at the end of the day, I decided to not keep this promise about passing out the candy. So at the end of the day, no one got candy. How would this make you feel?* (Children will hold up the frowning face.)

3. *I promise to let the class watch a television show this Friday. How does this make you feel?* (Children will hold up the smiley face.)

4. *Pretend that when Friday comes, I decided to not keep this promise. So on Friday, no one got to watch a television program. How would this make you feel?* (Children will hold up the frowning face.)

5. *When people keep their promises, how does that make you feel?* (Children will hold up the smiley face.)

6. *If someone does not keep his or her promises, how does this make you feel?* (Children will hold up the frowning face.)

▶ Tell the children:

Making and keeping promises is serious. You should never make a promise you do not intend to keep. When you break promises, you lose friends and people will not trust you. So it is important that when you make the decision to make a promise, it is a promise that you can keep. Another word for important *is* critical. *It is important to remember that making and keeping promises is a critical decision. This is true not only at your age, but throughout your whole life.*

CRITICAL DECISIONS © 2006 MAR✦CO PRODUCTS, INC. 1-800-448-2197

Story:

▸ Introduce the story by saying:

  Today we will be hearing a story about a rabbit that learns the importance of making the critical decision to keep her promises.

▸ Read *Rita Rabbit Decides To Keep Her Promises* (page 91-96).

Discussion Questions:

▸ Present the following questions to the children. Remind them of the importance of the critical decision of keeping their promises.

   1. *What should you decide about your promise in this situation? Your elderly neighbor asks you to shovel snow from her sidewalk and you promise her you will. But just as you get your shovel out to go over to your neighbor's house, a friend stops by and asks you to go sledding with him. What should you decide to do?* (You should decide to keep your promise. You should tell your friend that you promised to shovel your neighbor's sidewalk, so you cannot go sledding at this moment. You should keep your promise so your neighbor will still trust and believe in you and not be upset with you.)

   2. *What should you decide about your promise in this situation? Your friend asks you to help him with some problems he is having with his homework. Later, you regret your promise to help him because you do not think you will have any fun helping him. What should you decide to do?* (You should decide to keep your promise and help your friend. When you keep your promise, your friend will be able to trust you and will not be upset with you.)

   3. *What should you decide about your promise in this situation? You promised your little sister that you would share your candy bar with her. But when you took a bite, your candy bar tasted so good that you did not want to share it. What should you decide to do?* (You should decide to keep your promise and share your candy bar with your sister. When you keep your promise, your sister will be able to trust you and will not be upset with you.)

▶ For older/more advanced children, you may want to ask additional discussion questions. Say:

Sometimes it is difficult to keep a promise exactly as you have planned. Listen to the descriptions of the following situations and discuss what a person should decide to do in these difficult situations.

Present the following examples:

1. *Your teacher promises to take your class outside for a picnic. When the time comes to go outside, it starts to storm. What can the teacher decide to do to keep her promise the best she can in this situation?* (a. The teacher could explain that she could not take you outside because it is unsafe to be outside during a storm, but that you may have a picnic inside. The teacher could have you move your desks and have a picnic on the floor. b. The teacher could say she is sorry you cannot go outside for the picnic due to the rain, but that if it is not raining tomorrow, you may go out then.)

2. *Your parents promised they would take you to the movies. When the time came for your parents to take you to the movies, the theater was not showing a movie rated for children to watch. What could your parents decide to do to keep their promise the best they can?* (a. Your parents could explain why they cannot take you to the movies. The reason could be that the movies showing this week are not for children or are too scary or not interesting to children. They could offer to take you to rent a movie and maybe buy you some popcorn to eat at home. b. Your parents could explain why they cannot take you to the movies this week and promise to take you to see the next movie that is rated for children.)

3. *Your friend promised to take you to the circus this weekend with her family. Then your friend got sick and could not go. What can your friend do in this situation to keep her promise the best she can?* (Your friend can explain why she and her family cannot take you to the circus this weekend. It might not be good for your friend to be doing anything active because she needs to rest in order to get well. She could say that she and her family will invite you to do something else fun at a later date.)

Follow-Up Activities:

ACTIVITY #1

▶ This activity will help children better understand that keeping promises is a critical decision.

▶ Materials needed: Chalkboard and chalk for the leader.

▶ Write the word *promise* on the board. With the children, brainstorm sentences that include each letter in the word *promise.* This will help children develop their understanding of the importance of their keeping their promises. For example:

> **P**romises should be kept.
> **R**eally try to keep your promises.
> **O**nly make promises you intend to keep.
> **M**aking a promise is a critical decision.
> **I**f you must break a promise, explain why.
> **S**ay you are sorry if you break your promises.
> **E**veryone wants their friends to keep their promises.

ACTIVITY #2

▶ The purpose of this activity is to reinforce the importance of keeping promises through rewritten lyrics to a familiar song.

▶ Materials needed: None

▶ Sing the song below to the tune of *"Jingle Bells."*

> Keep your promises.
> Keep your promises.
> Keep them every day.
>
> Keep your promises.
> Keep your promises.
> Do what you say.

ACTIVITY #3

▸ The purpose of this activity is to help children realize the benefits of making the critical decision to keep their promises and also to help them see possible consequences of breaking promises.

▸ Materials needed: None

▸ Have the children role-play the following situations. Then discuss how the children felt in each situation.

Two children pretend to talk on the phone.

- Child A says, "I promise to call you back in a minute."
- The children pretend to hang up the phones, then Child A pretends to call Child B back.
- Child A says, "I kept my promise to call you back."
- Child B says, "Thank you."

Two children pretend to be doing homework.

- Child C says, "I don't understand this work."
- Child D says, "I'll be glad to help you when I finish mine."
- Child D works for a bit, then goes to help Child C.
- Child D says, "I kept my promise to help you."
- Child C says, " Thank you."

Other similar skits ideas are:

- One child promises another child to share his/her crayons.
- One child promises to help another child clean out his/her desk.
- One child promises to invite another child over to his/her house.
- One child promises to invite another child to his/her birthday party.
- One child promises to help another child tie his/her shoes.
- One child promises to help another child open his/her carton of milk.
- One child promises to share his/her snack with another child.
- One child promises to visit another child.

The children could also role-play these situations with the first child not keeping his/her promises.

RITA RABBIT DECIDES TO KEEP HER PROMISES

"Good morning," Mother said to Rita Rabbit. "I am glad you are awake. I have your favorite Carrot Crunch Cereal for you and your sister, but I don't have any milk.

"I need to borrow some milk from Ms. Cow across the field. Would you mind going and getting some for me? Your sister and I will set the table and wait for you to come back."

"Sure," answered Rita Rabbit. "I don't mind at all getting the milk. I love Carrot Crunch Cereal. I'll go get some milk and be right back."

"Do you promise to get the milk and come straight home?" asked Mother Rabbit.

"Yes, I promise," said Rita Rabbit.

"Thank you," said her mother.

Rita was hopping across the field to Ms. Cow's house when she spotted her friend Sally Sheep.

"Hi, Sally," said Rita to her buddy.

"Hi back at ya," replied Sally.

"What are you doing?" asked Rita Rabbit.

"Well, I'm having some trouble," confessed Sally. "I am having a very difficult time with my shoelaces. Both of them keep breaking when I try to tie them. I think I need some new ones. These must be too old to use any more. I'm getting a bit frustrated because I am supposed to go to basketball practice in about 30 minutes. If I don't have my sneakers fixed by practice time, I don't think I'll be able to play."

"Hey, don't worry. I just happen to have some new shoelaces at my house that I am not going to use. I'll bring them to you," said Rita happily. "Just stay put. I am going to borrow some milk from Ms. Cow. When I go home with the milk, I'll get your shoelaces. I promise."

"Great!" replied Sally Sheep. "I sure appreciate your helping me. Do you think you will be able to get them in time for me to get to basketball practice?"

"No problem," said Rita Rabbit. "I promise to have them to you in time so you won't miss your practice."

Sally Sheep breathed a sigh of relief, "Thanks a lot!"

Rita then went hopping on her way to Ms. Cow's house to get the milk. When she was almost there, she saw her friend Greta Groundhog.

"Hi, Greta," said Rita. "What are you doing?"

"Hi, Rita," said Greta Groundhog. "I am planning on having a great time this afternoon. I have new sandbox at home. I am just getting back from the store. I have all kinds of new sand toys here in my shopping bag. You ought to come over and play. We would have a great time together, and I'd let you use my new sand toys."

"Wow!" said Rita. "A new sandbox! I would love to play with you!"

Rita Rabbit remembered the favors she had promised to do, but she thought that her mother, her sister, and Sally Sheep wouldn't mind waiting a little while longer.

 CRITICAL DECISIONS © 2006 MAR✱CO PRODUCTS, INC. 1-800-448-2197

Well, a little while turned into a long while. Rita and Greta played and played and played.

Reader: Pause. Ask the children the following questions, then continue reading the story.

Should Rita Rabbit have gone to play with Greta Groundhog? (No.)

Why? (She promised to get the milk and shoelaces and now she is not keeping her promises.)

"Greta, I am so glad you asked me to come over! This sandbox is the greatest! Pass me that shovel and bucket again, please," said Rita. She was not thinking about the time or about what she had promised to do.

"Sure thing," said Greta Groundhog. "We can play a little longer. Then I'd like to go in and get something to eat. I'm hungry. I skipped my breakfast this morning because I was too excited to sit down and eat. Now it is almost lunch time."

The minute Greta said something about eating, Rita started remembering her promises to her mother, her sister, and Sally Sheep.

"Oh, my goodness!" shouted Rita Rabbit. "I promised to get milk and shoelaces a long time ago, and I didn't do what I promised I would do!"

"What are you talking about?" asked Greta.

"I'll have to explain later," answered Rita. "I have to go home right now!"

When Rita Rabbit got home, her house was full of animals. Ms. Cow, Mr. Rooster, Sally Sheep and most of her friends were there.

"What is everyone doing here?" asked Rita as she entered her kitchen.

"RITA!" her mother shouted when she saw her. "We have all been worried sick about you! None of us knew where you were. You promised to go to Ms. Cow's house and come right back. When you promise to do something, you should do it unless there is trouble of some kind. When you didn't come back, we thought you might be in some kind of trouble. We have been looking and looking for you!

"Rita Rabbit, since you did not keep your promise, we have been worried sick," her mother scolded. "And because you did not keep your promise, you caused your sister and me to miss our breakfast. Your behavior has the whole neighborhood upset!"

"And," said Sally Sheep, "you promised you would get me some shoelaces. You didn't, so I had to miss my basketball practice."

Ms. Cow, Mr. Rooster, and Sally Sheep worriedly exclaimed, "You had us scared to death! You need to realize that making promises is a critical decision and that it is important to keep the promises you make!"

Rita Rabbit then realized what a mess she had caused. Because she did not keep her promises, her mother and sister had missed their breakfast. Sally Sheep had missed her basketball practice, and Ms. Cow and Mr. Rooster and the other neighbors and friends had spent their morning being worried and upset.

Reader: Pause. Ask the children the following question, then continue reading the story.

What should Rita Rabbit do now that she realizes what a mess she has caused? (She should say she is sorry and make the critical decision to keep her promises from now on.)

Rita looked around at everyone and said, "I am very sorry for what I did. I can promise you that I have learned a lesson. I realize that making and keeping promises is a critical decision. From now on, I will always keep my promises. I am really sorry to have caused everyone so much worry."

"Thank heaven you are OK, Rita," said her mother.

Ms. Cow spoke up, "Well, we are all here and we all need something to eat. And since we have a whole new box of cereal and I can get us plenty of milk, how about having a *celebration breakfast*? We can celebrate that Rita Rabbit is OK and that she has decided to keep her promises."

Everyone cheered at that idea. Rita took a deep breath and said to Sally, "After breakfast, do you want me to practice basketball with you?"

Rita reached into a drawer and pulled out the shoelaces. "Here are the shoelaces I promised you. I really am sorry."

Sally smiled at Rita as she took the new shoelaces. "I'm glad you learned this good lesson. I am proud of you," said Sally Sheep.

"We all are!" chimed in all the animals.

Reader: Conclude the story by asking the children the following questions:

Do you think Rita will make the critical decision to keep her promises from now on? (Yes.)

Why? (She has learned that not keeping promises upsets people.)

THE CRITICAL DECISION TO
ACCEPT AND RESPECT PHYSICALLY OR MENTALLY CHALLENGED PEOPLE

Lesson Plan Objectives:

1. Read the story to the children for the purpose of teaching them about the importance of making the critical decision to treat mentally and physically challenged people with respect.

2. Discuss the questions before or after reading the story to encourage thinking/talking about the results of choosing to treat mentally and physically challenged people with respect.

3. Select one or more follow-up activities to give children practical experiences treating mentally and physically challenged people with respect.

☺☺☺☺ LESSON ☺☺☺☺

Introduction:

▶ Materials needed: Bandage for the leader.

▶ Enter the room with your arm bandaged. Then introduce the lesson by asking:

What might be difficult to do if I had a hurt and bandaged arm? (I might have trouble tying my shoes or I might need some help getting my lunch tray. Basically, I might need some assistance with things that involve using both hands.)

What would I be able to do whether or not I had a hurt and bandaged arm? (I still could teach and care for children. I would still be the same person I always was.)

Then say:

Some people in this world have something hurt or wrong with their bodies. They may have been born this way or they might have had an accident. People who are mentally challenged do not learn as quickly as others. Someone who is physically challenged may need to use a wheelchair. But people who are mentally or physically challenged are still people just like you and me. They still have the same feelings as you and me and they can be wonderful friends.

Not accepting people because they are different from you is a serious mistake. It is important to accept all people for who they are, not because they look and act just like you. When you accept all people you make the decision to be a respectful person. This is a serious decision. Another word for serious is critical. It is important to make the critical decision to treat all people respectfully.

Story:

▶ Introduce the story by saying:

Today you are going to hear a story about two children who know that what really counts is a person's heart, not any possible differences. In our story, these children make the critical decision to treat all people respectfully.

▶ Read *Heart Of Gold* (pages 104-107).

Discussion Questions:

▶ Present the following questions to the children. Remind them of the importance of the critical decision of treating all people respectfully.

1. *What does it mean to say that a person is mentally or physically challenged?* (It means that a part of his/her body does not work as well as other people's.)

2. *Can you be friends with a person who is mentally or physically challenged?* (Yes.)

3. *How can you be friends with someone who is mentally or physically challenged?* (You can be friends with this person just like you can be friends with anyone. A mentally or physically challenged person has the same feelings as anyone and can be a wonderful friend.)

4. *If you have a friend who uses a wheelchair, what are some things you can do together?* (You can go to the movies, talk on the phone, draw, laugh, go shopping, watch TV, play basketball, etc. Your friend may need some assistance at times, but you can do almost anything together.)

5. *If you have a friend who is blind, what are some things you can do together?* (You can talk on the phone, listen to music, play musical instruments, read books, laugh, tell jokes to each other, go walking, etc. Your friend may need some assistance at times, but you can do just about anything together.)

6. *How are mentally or physically challenged people the same as everyone else?* (We all have the same feelings, like to have fun, want to have friends, have hobbies, need exercise, need love, etc. Mentally and physically challenged people and people without these disabilities are alike in more ways than they are different.

Follow-Up Activities:

ACTIVITY #1

▶   This activity will help children learn that many famous and successful people had mental or physical challenges.

▶   Materials needed: Book or story about a famous person who is mentally or physically challenged for the leader.

▶   Read a book about a famous person who was mentally or physically challenged. For example:

- Helen Keller: She was blind, deaf, and mute, but she did not give up. With the help of her teacher, Anne Sullivan, she lived a very inspirational and successful life.

- President Franklin D. Roosevelt: He was the 32nd president of the United States. Because he contracted polio, he spent part of his life in a wheelchair.

- Ludwig van Beethoven: He was a musician who wrote beautiful music after he became deaf.

ACTIVITY #2

▶ This activity will help the children realize the challenges that physically challenged people face every day and will, hopefully, help them appreciate the efforts these people put forth to complete the tasks of daily living.

▶ Materials needed: Wheelchair, crutches, sling, finger splint, and blindfold for the groups.

▶ Divide the class into five groups of about five people. Give each group one of the props. Have each person use the prop to complete one of the activities listed below.

- Sharpen a pencil.
- Open a door.
- Carry books across the room.
- Clean out and straighten a desk.
- Erase the board.

▶ After each of the children has had time to complete each activity, allow time for everyone to discuss the problems and solutions each task involved.

ACTIVITY #3

▶ This activity will help the children make the critical decision to treat physically challenged people with respect in a real-life situation.

▶ Materials needed: None

▶ Invite a guest speaker who, despite physical challenges, has succeeded in reaching his/her goals to speak to the class.

▸ Some questions that the class could ask the guest are:

1. *What are some challenges you have been able to overcome?*

2. *Do you feel that people think of you and treat you differently due to your situation?*

3. *Who has helped you through difficult times?*

4. *What advice do you have for us as we face challenges each day?*

5. *What inspired you to meet your challenges head-on and not give up?*

ACTIVITY #4

▸ This activity will teach children to make the critical decision to know that what counts is whether a person is kind and good to others.

▸ Materials needed: Two plastic eggs (one in perfect shape and the other broken), candy, and pebbles for the leader.

▸ Place candy in the broken egg. Place pebbles in the perfectly shaped egg.

▸ Show the children the eggs and ask:

Which egg would you rather have? (Most will respond that they would rather have the pretty egg.)

▸ After the children respond, show them what is inside the eggs. (Candy in the broken one, and pebbles in the perfectly shaped one.)

▸ Then ask:

Which egg would you rather have now? (The children will want the broken egg.)

Why? (Because they like what is inside it.)

▸ Tell the children:

Just as you judged the eggs by what they looked like on the outside, sometimes people judge each other by looks alone. Remember this lesson: Don't judge people based on how they look. What matters is if a person has a loving heart.

▸ If there is enough candy, pass it to the children to eat or give each child a plastic egg filled with candy to help them remember the lesson.

ACTIVITY #5

▸ (Note: Before this activity, check to see if anyone is allergic to eggs.)

▸ This activity will give the children a way to remember that making the critical decision to respect mentally and physically challenged people is the right thing to do.

▸ Materials needed: One hard-boiled egg, crayons, and stickers (optional) for each child.

▸ Distribute a hard-boiled egg, crayons, and stickers (if you are using them) to each child. Have the children color their eggs with crayons.

▸ When the children have finished coloring their eggs, have them take turns showing their eggs to the class. Compliment each child for a decorating job done well.

▸ Tell the class that even though the eggs are different on the outside, they are the same on the inside.

▸ Have the children peel their eggs and look at the white part of the egg and the gold-centers. Compare the eggs to show that they are the same on the inside. Then children who are not allergic to eggs may eat their eggs if they want to.

▶ After eating the eggs, say:

Just like your eggs, people may be different on the outside, but inside, we are all are the same.

No matter what we look like on the outside, each person has the same feelings. We all need food, water, shelter, and love.

People with mental or physical challenges should not be judged by their challenges. What matters is if a person has a loving heart.

Remember: Mentally and physically challenged people have much in common with people who do not have such challenges.

HEART OF GOLD

"Come on, Hope! I have hidden some eggs for you in our back yard. You haven't learned about egg hunts yet, but you are old enough now for me to teach you. Come on now, Hope. We are going to have a lot of fun," exclaimed Mother.

Hope toddled outside with her mother. When Mother gave her a basket, Hope grinned from ear to ear.

"OK, Hope, let's find those eggs!" said Mother.

Mother led Hope to a bush where two shiny eggs were hidden.

Hope, squealed with delight. "Oooo! Pretty!" she said as she pointed and picked up the sparkling-colored eggs from under the bush.

"Yes, they are very pretty, Hope. I put glitter on these eggs and they shine like the sun," said Mother as she helped Hope lay the eggs gently into her basket.

Then Mother led Hope to her playhouse, where more eggs were hidden.

About this time, Hope's big brother came home from school. He ran to see what his sister and his mother were doing.

"We are hunting eggs, Brian. Do you want to join us?" asked Mother.

"Sure I do!" said Brian as he started looking around the playhouse.

"Hey! I found some over here. Come here, Hope. Look at what I found," said Brian.

Hope moved around the playhouse as quickly as she could. Her mother stayed close to her.

Brian showed his sister the eggs he had found by the playhouse.

"No! No!" cried Hope.

"No?" questioned Brian and Mother.

"Shiny eggs!" said Hope. "Want shiny eggs!"

"Oh, my!" laughed Mother. "Hope and I just found two eggs decorated with shiny glitter, and these eggs do not have glitter in their coloring. I think Hope wants all the eggs she finds to be shiny ones."

Brian laughed, too, and said, "OK, Hope, let's put these back and look for some more shiny ones."

Then Mother saw a great opportunity to teach a lesson to her children. She said, "Come close to me, children. I want to show you something."

Both Hope and Brian moved close to their mother. "Watch this," said Mother. She peeled the shell off one of the shiny eggs, then peeled the shell off of one of the eggs that wasn't shiny. She put the eggs behind her back, then brought them out again.

"Which one do you think was the shiny one?" asked Mother.

"We can't tell now," said Brian. "They don't have the outside on them any more."

"That's right," said Mother. "The color on the outside was different from the other egg, but what is under the shells of the eggs is the same."

Reader: Pause. Ask the children the following question, then continue reading the story.

How are people like these eggs? (People may look different on the outside, but we are the same on the inside.)

"Now," said Mother, "let me show you something else." Slowly, she parted the two eggs to show their golden centers. "Can you tell which one was the shiny one by looking in the middle of them?" she asked.

"No," said Brian and Hope.

"Right again!" said Mother. "In the middle, both eggs have the same golden center."

"Did you know that a good lesson can be learned from this experiment. The lesson you have learned about these eggs can apply to people as well," said Mother.

"How?" asked Brian.

"Well," said Mother, "the way people look on the outside does not show whether they are good or bad people. The important part is how people act from the inside—inside their hearts. No matter what people look like on the outside, if they have love, kindness, patience, and understanding they have something golden in them just like the eggs."

"What?" asked Brian curiously.

"Why, they have a heart of gold," said Mother smiling. "And no one is better than a person with a heart of gold."

Brian smiled wisely, knowing what his mother was teaching him. "I agree," he said.

Then Brian helped his mother unlock her wheelchair. He followed her and Hope to the next place, knowing they would find more gold.

Reader: Conclude the story by asking the children the following question:

Why was it important to Mother for Brian and Hope to know about not judging people based on how they look? (It was very important to Mother that Hope and Brian learn this lesson because she was physically challenged and used a wheelchair. She wanted her children to know that the most important thing is not how a person looks on the outside, but whether he/she has a loving heart on the inside. She wanted her children to make the critical decision to treat mentally and physically challenged people respectfully.)

THE CRITICAL DECISION TO
HELP KEEP OUR WORLD CLEAN

Lesson Plan Objectives:

1. Read the story to the children for the purpose of teaching them about the importance of making the critical decision to help keep our world clean.

2. Discuss the questions before or after reading the story to encourage thinking/talking about the results of choosing to help keep our world clean.

3. Select one or more follow-up activities to give children practical experiences in helping to keep our world clean.

⊚⊚⊚⊚ LESSON ⊚⊚⊚⊚

Introduction:

▸   Materials needed: Pictures of landscapes for each group. (Calendars often include beautiful landscapes.)

▸   Divide the children into groups and give each group some pictures of landscapes.

▸   Have the children discuss within their groups what they see that is beautiful.

▸   After the children have had time to view all the pictures, ask them to share with the whole class what they saw in the pictures that they thought was pretty.

▸   Ask the children:

   Did you see anything in these pictures that made the landscapes look unclean? (No.)

▶ Then say:

These pictures are part of our world. In order for trees, flowers, grass, bushes, and other beautiful things in nature to stay beautiful, it is important to keep our world clean. In fact, it is critical. Critical *is another word for* important *or* serious, *and it is critical that we all make the decision to do our best to protect nature. This is a critical decision that everyone must make.*

Story:

▶ Introduce the story by saying:

Today you are going to hear a story about some animals that live in a forest. These animals make a critical decision to help keep their world clean.

If you listen carefully, this story can help you understand how you can help keep the world clean.

▶ Read *Bear Teaches About Helping The Environment* (pages 113-117).

Discussion Questions:

▶ Present the following questions to the children. Remind them of the importance of the critical decision to keep our world clean.

1. *What is pollution?* (Pollution is anything that causes our world to be unclean.)

2. *How does our world get polluted?* (Pollution occurs when people throw their trash on our land, people throw their trash into our water, smoke from cars and factories pollutes our air, etc.)

3. *What does* recycling *mean?* (It means using something again instead of throwing it away.)

Then give the children the following examples of ways we can recycle. Say:

Instead of throwing our clothes away after we outgrow them, we can give them to someone they fit so they can be used again.

Instead of throwing paper away after using just the front, we can use the back, too.

We can turn our newspapers, glass, and plastic products into a recycling center so they can be processed to use again for new newspapers, glass, and plastic products.

Instead of throwing old books away, we can donate them to a daycare center, nursery school, or library.

Instead of throwing our pencils and crayons away when they get a little short, we could keep using them.

Continue the discussion questions by asking:

4. *How can recycling keep our world cleaner?* (If we use things again instead of throwing them away, then there will not be as much trash in our world.)

5. *How can we keep our world from getting polluted?* (We can keep our world from getting polluted by putting our trash into trash cans instead of on the land; keeping our trash in a bag instead of throwing it into the water; carpooling, riding bikes, or walking so there will not be as much air pollution; and recycling whenever possible.)

6. *Who or what is affected by pollution?* (People, animals, insects ... every living thing is affected in a some way by pollution.)

Then give the children the following examples of the effects of pollution. Say:

People, animals, and insects cannot breathe as well when there is smoke in the air.

Pollution in our water causes fish to get sick. Since people eat fish, they could get sick, too.

When there is pollution on the land, the insects eat something unclean. A bird could eat these insects and get sick. People who eat these birds could get sick, too.

Pollution affects everything and everybody in a bad way.

Follow–Up Activities:

ACTIVITY #1

▸ This activity will help the children more clearly understand how pollution hurts our environment and hurts them, too. It will help children to understand the importance of making the critical decision to keep our world clean.

▸ Materials needed: Piece of unlined paper, crayons, and pencil for each child.

▸ Distribute paper, crayons, and a pencil to each child. Instruct the children to turn the paper sideways and draw a line down the middle. Have them label one half *Land That Is Polluted* and label the other half *Land That Is Not Polluted.*

▸ Have the children draw and color the same landscape on each half of the page. Have one picture show no pollution in the land and have the other picture show lots of pollution in the land.

▸ When the children have completed their drawings, have them share what they have drawn with each other and discuss how pollution caused the land to look unclean. (Note: These pictures would make a good bulletin board display.)

ACTIVITY #2

▸ This activity will give the children real-life information on the harmful effects of pollution.

▸ Materials needed: None

▸ Invite a guest speaker, such as a park ranger, police officer, or someone from an environmental agency to talk to the class.

▸ Have the guest speaker tell the class about the importance of not polluting our world.

ACTIVITY #3

▸ This activity gives the children practical experience in making the critical decision to keep our world clean.

▸ Materials needed: None

▸ Plan for the children to do something together that will help keep our world beautiful. Some things the children could do are:

- Pick up the trash left on the playground after recess. Instruct the children to not pick up broken glass or anything that could hurt them.

- Have the children buy a tree and plant it on the school grounds.

- Have the children make and illustrate signs that say things like: *Don't Litter, Help Keep Our World Clean, Recycle,* or *Pollution Can Make You Sick.* Display the posters.

- Ask the children to bring old newspapers and/or empty soda cans to your room. Take a field trip to a recycling center, donate your items, and learn how a recycling center works.

BEAR TEACHES ABOUT HELPING THE ENVIRONMENT

Bear stretched a big-bear stretch as he started to leave his cave. "Boy, that was a good winter's nap," he said as he yawned and stretched again.

When he reached the entrance to his cave, he noticed a big mess! "My, my, my!" exclaimed Bear. "What has happened here?"

Bear looked around outside his cave. He saw trash, trash, and more trash!

"This isn't how my yard looked when I went in for my nap," said Bear, feeling quite upset. "I need to find out what is going on here."

Just then he noticed his friends. They were having a picnic in the park area.

"Hey, guys!" shouted Bear.

"Hey," responded his friends. "It's Bear! Yeah! We have missed you. Aren't you a bit late waking up this year?"

"Yeah, I guess I am," answered Bear. "I was really sleeping well. What are you all up to?"

"We are having a picnic," said Deer. "Come and join us."

"Well, I must say I am truly hungry. I always like to eat a lot when I first get up. What do you have?"

"We have just about anything you want," replied Rabbit. "Just dig in and help yourself!"

Bear did dig in. He ate and ate and ate!

"This was a great picnic," said Bear as he finished up one last sandwich.

"It sure was," agreed Fox. "I am so full!"

"We are all going to go swimming in the watering hole. Would you like to join us, Bear?"

"I sure would," said Bear. "Thanks!"

"Come on then," shouted his friends. "We'll race you there."

CRITICAL DECISIONS © 2006 MAR+CO PRODUCTS, INC. 1-800-448-2197

"Hey," said Bear. "Aren't you going to clean up the mess from our picnic?"

Reader: Pause. Ask the children the following questions, then continue reading the story.

Do you think deciding to clean up the picnic mess is a critical decision? (Yes.)

Why? (If the mess is not cleaned up, the woods will become polluted and unclean.)

"What do you mean, Bear?" asked Squirrel.

"Well, just look around," said Bear. "There is trash everywhere from our picnic. Don't you think we should clean it up?"

"Well, we never have," said Turkey.

Bear looked all around. "I can tell you haven't. Just look around at what a mess this area of the woods has become. Did you make all this mess?"

The animals began to look around. They saw paper flying around in the wind and empty cans scattered everywhere. It really did look bad. Trash was everywhere and Turkey noticed a stinky smell, too.

"Gosh, Bear, I never paid much attention to the mess we have been causing," admitted Fox. "We have not been very good to our woods, have we?"

"No, we have not," agreed Squirrel.

"I agree. Everything is a mess," said Deer.

Reader: Pause. Ask the children the following question, then continue reading the story.

What should the animals do to make the woods cleaner? (They should clean up the mess they made and not make any more messes.)

"I agree with Bear. It is our responsibility to clean up what we mess up," said Squirrel.

"You are all right. We live in these woods, and the woods are part of our world. Our teachers taught us that helping to keep our world clean is a critical decision everyone must make," said Bear. "I also learned that pollution not only makes our world look bad, but can also cause us to get sick."

"You are right," said the animals. "We need to clean up everything. Let's get started."

"I am so glad we are deciding clean up. We can swim after everything is back to the way it should be," said Bear.

The animals worked the rest of the morning and the better part of the afternoon, picking up and making everything look great again. And when they were finished, they felt very proud of themselves.

"Boy!" exclaimed Bear proudly, as he looked around again. "Everything looks great now!"

The animals looked around. This time, they saw butterflies flying around in the air and the beautiful grass blowing in the wind. They could now smell the fresh, sweet flowers. Everything was as it should be. Everything was gorgeous!

Reader: Pause. Ask the children the following question, then continue reading the story.

How do you think the animals feel now? (They feel proud of themselves because they made the critical decision to help keep the world clean and they have made their woods look beautiful again.)

"We sure have made a positive difference here, haven't we, Bear?" asked the animals.

"We sure have," replied Bear. "Since we decided to take care of our woods, everything looks so much better and we won't have to worry about getting sick due to the pollution we were causing. I am really proud of us."

"Now how about a dip in the cool, clean watering hole?" asked Deer.

"You're on for that! Yeah!" said Bear. "Let's go!"

The animals spent the rest of the evening swimming and enjoying having a pretty place to play. It was a good day, and everyone learned a great lesson about the importance of making the critical decision to help keep the world clean.

THE CRITICAL DECISION TO DECIDE TO HAVE GOOD SELF-ESTEEM

Lesson Plan Objectives:

1. Read the story to the children for the purpose of teaching them about the importance of making the critical decision to have good self-esteem (thinking good, positive thoughts about yourself).

2. Discuss the questions before or after reading the story to encourage thinking/talking about the results of choosing or not choosing to have a good self-esteem.

3. Select one or more follow-up activities to give children practical experiences in developing good self-esteem.

 **LESSON**

Introduction:

▶   Begin the lesson by telling the children what it means to have good self-esteem and why having good self-esteem is important. Say:

> *Having good self-esteem means you think good, positive thoughts about yourself.*
>
> *It is important to have good self-esteem so you will be happy. If you think bad thoughts about yourself a lot of the time, it will be hard for you to be happy.*
>
> *Another word for* critical *is* important. *It is critical to have good self-esteem. You develop good self-esteem when you decide to continually think or say good things about yourself. Always remember that having good self-esteem is a critical or important decision you must make for yourself.*

▸ Instruct the children to repeat after you, verse by verse, a poem that will help them develop good self-esteem.

I'm very special, (Have the children repeat each line after you.)
And nice as I can be.
I'm very smart,
And I really like me.

I have friends who like me.
Yes, they do.
I'm glad I'm me,
And this is true!

Story:

▸ Introduce the story by saying:

Today you are going to hear a story about a character that makes the critical decision to have good self-esteem. If you listen carefully, this story can help you understand how to have a better self-esteem, too.

▸ Read *A Star Is Born* (pages 124-129).

Discussion Questions:

▸ Present the following questions to the children. Remind them of the importance of the critical decision to have good self-esteem.

1. *What must we do in order to have good self-esteem?* (In order to have good self-esteem, we must think good thoughts about ourselves a lot of the time.)

2. *What are some good thoughts that we could think about ourselves in order to have good self-esteem?* (a. We could think about what we do well. b. We could think about what we are thankful for. c. We could try to focus on good things that happen to us during the day.)

3. *Why is it better to think good thoughts about yourself than to think bad thoughts about yourself?* (It is better to think good thoughts about yourself because good thoughts will help you to be happier.)

4. *What are some characteristics of a person with good self-esteem?* (A person who has good self-esteem seems happy most of the time and does not let unpleasant things get him/her down for very long.)

5. *What are some characteristics of a person with poor self-esteem?* (A person who has a poor self-esteem seems sad most of the time and lets unpleasant things keep him/her feeling down.)

6. *Would you rather be a person with a good self-esteem or a person with poor self-esteem?* (Good self-esteem.)

    Why? (Because a person with good self-esteem is happier than a person with poor self-esteem.)

Follow-Up Activities:

ACTIVITY #1

▸   This activity will help the children focus on themselves and start to think of the good qualities they possess. This will encourage them to make the critical decision to have good self-esteem.

▸   Materials needed: Mirror for each group of five children.

▸   Divide the class into groups of about five children. Give each group a hand mirror. Then say:

    Take turns holding the mirror. When it is your turn to hold the mirror, look into the mirror and repeat each verse after I say it aloud. Those of you who are not holding the mirror should also say the verses. The child holding the mirror should be watching himself or herself in the mirror.

▸ Repeat the verses in the *Introduction.*

> *I'm very special,* (Have the children repeat each line after you.)
> *And nice as I can be.*
> *I'm very smart,*
> *And I really like me.*
>
> *I have friends who like me.*
> *Yes, they do.*
> *I'm glad I'm me,*
> *And this is true!*

▸ Repeat the verse enough times so every child in every group has an opportunity to hold the mirror.

▸ (Optional) After each child has repeated the verses while looking into the mirror, teach the children to sing the verses to the tune of "*I'm a Little Teapot.*" Singing will help the children memorize the verses. You may want to sing this little song at the beginning and at the end of each day to encourage the children to start developing good self-esteem.

ACTIVITY #2

▸ This activity will help the children notice good things about themselves.

▸ Materials needed: Paper and pencil for each child. Chalkboard and chalk for the leader.

▸ Distribute paper and a pencil to each child.

▸ Tell the children that you are going to ask each of them to compliment themselves.

▸ Have the children write their names on the paper. Then tell them to write or draw some things they do well. In order to get the children thinking, you may wish to write and/or draw some examples on the board.

▶ Write or illustrate the following on the board:

- I am a good friend.
- I am good at basketball or another sport.
- I am good at taking care of animals.
- I am good at organizing things.
- I am good at math or another subject.
- I am good at helping people.
- I am good at drawing.
- I am good at building things.
- I am good at cleaning the house.
- I am a good listener.
- I am a good sister/brother.
- I am a good son/daughter.
- I am a good granddaughter/grandson.
- I am a good neighbor.

▶ After the children have written or drawn some things they do well, collect their papers. If time allows, make a note on each one saying how proud you are of the child or write something else you have noticed that each child does well. Return the papers and notice the joy of the children when they see what you have written to them. (Note: Younger children may say what they do well, and you may comment orally about how proud you are of them.)

ACTIVITY #3

▶ This activity gives the children immediate feedback about the positive things they see in themselves.

▶ Materials needed: Paper and pencil for each child.

▶ Distribute paper and a pencil to each child. Ask each child to write or draw at least one thing he/she did well during the school day.

▶ Collect the papers and read them. You may choose to write a note to each child.

▶ Return the papers to the children.

▶ Repeat the activity several times in order to encourage the children to think about what they do well during the day. This activity will help children focus on the positive things about themselves and develop better self-esteem.

(Note: You may want to let the children make a personal *Memory Book* out of these papers and illustrate some pages as a remembrance of the good things they have accomplished.)

▶ For younger children, you could ask out loud what they did well that day and let each child answer your question. Another possibility is to have each younger child draw a picture of what he/she did well each day. These pictures could be made into a picture book as a reminder of all the wonderful things each child has done.

 # A STAR IS BORN

A long time ago, a big lesson was learned from a little apple. Listen carefully and see if you can learn the lesson, too.

"Hooo, Hooo," said Wise Old Owl as he landed on the branch of an apple tree.

"Hooo, Hooo, yourself," Little Red Apple said gloomily.

Little Red Apple's tone of voice told Wise Old Owl that something was wrong. Wise Old Owl liked Little Red Apple and wanted to find out how to help her, so he said, "Little Red Apple, you don't sound very chipper today. What's wrong?"

"I don't feel very happy this evening. I guess you could say I'm kind of 'blue' instead of perky red," Little Red Apple said sadly.

"Well, dooooooo tell me. What is making you feel so blue?" asked Wise Old Owl.

"It all began a few evenings ago. I was just hanging around here in my tree, just like I'm doing now, and I began to notice how beautiful the stars were. Just look at them, Wise Old Owl! See how they shine through the darkness? Do you see how lovely they are? They look like thousands of flickering candles. I know that stars are not only beautiful to look at, they are very useful, too. They give light to the world at night and help travelers know which direction they are traveling. Oh, Wise Old Owl, I'm blue because I wish I were a star instead of a measly red apple. If I were a star, I'd be happy all the time. I would be pretty and useful," said Little Red Apple.

Wise Old Owl listened carefully to what Little Red Apple had to say. Then he tilted back his head and laughed!

"Why are you laughing at me?" cried Little Red Apple. "You aren't making me feel any better at all!"

"I'm sorry, Little Red Apple. I wasn't laughing because you are sad. I was laughing because I can't believe you don't know … "

"Know what?" interrupted Little Red Apple. "What is worth knowing?"

"Why, Little Red Apple, you should know that *every* apple is a star. If you look deep enough, you will see that you are a wonderful star, too."

"What do you mean?" asked Little Red Apple. "I am not a star. I don't shine in the sky or help travelers know their directions."

"I guess I need to explain myself, don't I?" asked Wise Old Owl. "To begin with, you are right that you don't live way up in the sky, you can't give off a bright light, and you would probably get travelers very mixed up with their directions. But Little Red Apple, I promise that if you look inside yourself, you will see that you *are* a star. Let me help you. To begin, please try to name some things you can do."

"What? I am very confused, Wise Old Owl. Why do I need to tell *you* some things *I* can do?" Little Red Apple asked curiously.

"Just trust me, Little Red Apple. Remember that I am very wise and I know what I'm doing. Now, come on, it is critical that you decide to tell me some things you can do," replied Wise Old Owl.

Reader: Pause. Ask the children the following question, then continue reading the story.

Why do you think Wise Old Owl thinks it is critical for Little Red Apple to name things she does well? (Wise Old Owl knows Little Red Apple will be happier because she will be thinking of things she can do, instead of things that she can't do.)

Little Red Apple knew the owl was very wise, so she decided to do what he asked her to do.

"OK, OK, I'll try. Let's see. Hmmmmm. Ahhhhhhhh. Let me think … Hmmmmm … OK, OK, I just thought of something … I help decorate this tree. A little girl once commented on how pretty this tree was and I couldn't help but think I had a little part in making this tree pretty. It seemed like she was looking at me when she said that compliment," smiled Little Red Apple.

"Good, good, Little Red Apple! That's one great thing about you. Even I notice, when I am flying above, what a pretty tree this is. And I agree that your bright red color does help make this tree pretty," said Wise Old Owl. Now tell me something else that you do well."

"I don't think I can think of anything else," said Little Red Apple.

"Of course you can," said Wise Old Owl. "Come on now, think of something else."

"OK, OK, I just thought of something else. I've been told that apples are very delicious, and people like fixing us in pies and cakes and even covering us with caramel," Little Red Apple said proudly.

"Keep going, Little Red Apple. You are doing great! Tell me something else you do well," urged Wise Old Owl.

"OK," said Little Red Apple, feeling happier and happier. "I am a good friend. Grey Squirrel comes to visit me almost every day and you come to see me, too. I think we have a good time together."

Reader: Pause. Ask the children the following questions, then continue reading the story.

Do you think Little Red Apple is developing better self-esteem? (Yes.)

Why? (She is developing better self-esteem because she is thinking good things about herself.)

"Yes, you are right, Little Red Apple. You are a wonderful friend of mine. I do enjoy our times together, and I know Grey Squirrel enjoys your company, too. I can hear you both chatting and laughing sometimes when I fly by," said Wise Old Owl.

"Also," continued Little Red Apple, "people say apples keep them healthy. I have heard that an apple a day keeps the doctor away!"

"Great, Little Red Apple! You do many things well. You realize now that just like the stars, you are pretty. You help decorate this fine tree. You are useful like the stars. You give people something healthy and delicious to eat. You are a super friend, too," said Wise Old Owl.

"But," continued Wise Old Owl, "you are still not seeing that you are a star. You must look very deep. Most of the time, the great qualities that make us stars are deep inside of us instead of on the outside. So look deep within yourself and tell me what you find."

Little Red Apple did as she was told, then said, "Oh! My seeds! I have heard that people sometimes make beautiful necklaces by stringing apple seeds together."

"You are right about that, Little Red Apple. That is another wonderful thing about you. But look closer and deeper to see that you are a *star*," instructed Wise Old Owl.

Little Red Apple looked as deep as she could and … there it was! Little Red Apple could hardly believe it. Way deep in the middle part of her was the shape of a star!

"Oh, my! Oh, my!" shouted Little Red Apple. "I see a star in me. Why, all along, I was a star and didn't even know it. Thank you so much for helping me see that I am a star, too!" Little Red Apple said thankfully. "I am deciding right now to not be blue because I have thought of good things about myself instead of bad things. I see now that I really and truly am a star."

"Super!" said Wise Old Owl. "You made the critical decision to think good things about yourself and that will always help you have good self-esteem. This means you won't be focusing on bad things about yourself any more. You will be focusing on good things about yourself. I am very glad you see that you are a wonderful star. And now that you

 CRITICAL DECISIONS © 2006 MAR•CO PRODUCTS, INC. 1-800-448-2197

know you are a star, you can help others have good self-esteem by helping them see the good things in them. Everyone is a star. They just have to realize how special they are."

Little Red Apple was happier than she had ever thought she could be. She thanked Wise Old Owl as he flew into the night sky. Little Red Apple loved knowing that she was a star.

Reader: Conclude the story by telling the children that there really is a star in every apple. Show them an apple or tell them that they will get to see the inside of an apple tomorrow.

When you have the apple, lay it on its side so the stem is sticking out on the side. Then cut the apple down the middle. One half of the apple will have the stem sticking out of the side. Show the children the star shape in each half of the apple.

You could bring a bag of apples and cut and peel sections of the apples for each child to eat.

These activities will help the children remember this story and remember to have good self-esteem.

THE CRITICAL DECISION TO
CHOOSE TO HAVE GOOD FEELINGS

Lesson Plan Objectives:

1. Read the story to the children for the purpose of teaching them about the importance of making the critical decision to have good feelings.

2. Discuss the questions before or after reading the story to encourage thinking/talking about the results of choosing to have good feelings.

3. Select one or more follow-up activities to give children practical experiences in choosing to have good feelings.

 **LESSON**

Introduction:

▸ Materials needed: Chalkboard and chalk for the leader.

▸ Begin the lesson by asking the children to use facial expressions to act out the feeling words you will be saying out loud. Say the following words:

- *happy* (Children could smile.)
- *sad* (Children could frown.)
- *worried* (Children could wrinkle eyebrows.)
- *scared* (Children could hide faces behind hands.)
- *sleepy* (Children could yawn.)
- *frustrated* (Children could tighten their lips.)
- *proud* (Children could sit up straight and smile.)
- *confused* (Children could tilt heads to the side.)
- *excited* (Children could raise eyebrows and smile.)

Story:

▶ Introduce the story by saying:

You are going to hear a story about a little lion that has a lot of different feelings, some wanted and some unwanted. He is going to decide to have good feelings, because when he has good feelings, he feels better. When he has bad feelings, he does not feel very good at all. This is a critical decision, because it is important to try and feel good. If you listen carefully, the story can teach you how to decide to have good feelings, too.

▶ Read *The Feelings Of Little Lion* (pages 135-140).

Discussion Questions:

▶ Present the following questions to the children. Remind them of the importance of the critical decision to have good feelings.

1. *Name some feelings you would not want to keep for very long.* (Sadness, anger, frustration, confusion, etc.)

2. *Name some feelings that you would want to keep for a long time.* (Happiness, calmness, peacefulness, thankfulness, etc.)

3. *Can you decide to replace your unwanted feelings with feelings you do want?* (Yes.) *How?*

   Write *W.I.N.* in large letters on the chalkboard. Then point to each letter and explain the following steps to help the children decide to have good feelings.

   W What is the feeling you are having?

   I Is it a feeling you want to keep? If yes, then great! If no, go to the next step.

   N Need to think of feelings that could replace unwanted feelings and choose one that is more positive.

▸ Using the *W.I.N.* steps, guide the children in a discussion of how they could change an *unwanted* feeling into a *wanted* feeling in the following situation. Say:

> *Your sister accidentally drops jelly from her sandwich onto your pants. You feel really angry with her.*
>
> *How could you change your feelings in this situation?*
>
> **W** *What is the feeling that you are having?* (Anger.)
>
> **I** *Is it a feeling you want to keep for very long?* (No.)
>
> **N** *Need to think of feelings that could replace unwanted feelings and choose one that is more positive.* (Calmness.)

Then say:

> *You could decide to be calm. You would be surprised how much easier it is to reach a good decision when you are calm.*

Follow-Up Activities:

ACTIVITY #1

▸ This activity will help the children know that any feeling they have is okay. Remind them that there are many feelings they don't want to have for long periods of time. When they have those feelings, they must make the critical decision to have good feelings in order to be happy and content.

▸ Materials needed: None

▸ Using the *W.I.N.* steps, guide the children in a discussion about how they could change an unwanted feeling into a wanted feeling in the following situation:

> *It is raining outside and you had planned on playing with your friends at the baseball field. Since you cannot play outside, you are feeling sad.*

W *What is the feeling that you are having?* (Sadness.)

I *Is it a feeling you want to keep?* (No.)

N *Need to think of feelings that could replace unwanted feelings and choose one that is more positive.* (Happiness.)

Then say:

> *You could decide to be happy that it is raining because this will give you time for an indoor project, such as playing a video game, writing a letter, drawing, calling a friend, or organizing your toys or clothes.*

▸ If time permits, you could present additional situations and help the children work through the *W.I.N.* steps for each situation given. Examples of situations are:

- You could feel confused about (<u>NAME SOMETHING BEING LEARNED IN CLASS</u>), then decide to feel determined to learn how to do it.

- You could feel shy about talking with someone, then decide to feel determined to speak to that person.

- You could feel embarrassed that you fell, then decide to laugh with your friends about your fall.

(Note: The leader could divide older or more advanced children into groups to discuss the *W.I.N.* steps for the situations listed above.)

ACTIVITY #2

▸ This activity will help the children understand that they have feelings all the time and every feeling is okay.

▸ Materials needed: None

▸ Teach the children the following song to the tune of *"Camptown Races."*

> *Feelings are very good.*
> *Feelings, feelings.*
> *They help us to be understood*
> *By our friends each day.*
>
> *We feel in the morning*
> *We feel in the night*
> *We have our feelings all the time*
> *And that is just all right.*

ACTIVITY #3

▸ This activity will give the children insight into many different kinds of feelings and remind them that some of the feelings they have they would not want to keep for long periods of time. When they have those feelings, they must make the critical decision to have good feelings in order to be happy or content.

▸ Materials needed: 3 x 5 cards and a pen for the leader.

▸ Write one feeling word on each card and stack the cards face-down in a pile. Possible words include: *happy, sad, confused, angry, excited, scared, bored, calm, jealous, hateful, curious, patient, embarrassed, tickled, crazy, cranky, frustrated, guilty, surprised,* and *content.*

▸ Have a child (or group of children) draw a card, then try to act out the feeling word written on the card.

▸ The rest of the children try to guess the feeling being acting out, then tell if this is a feeling they would like to have.

THE FEELINGS OF LITTLE LION

Daddy Lion was sitting in the den when Little Lion came through the door. "How was your day at school today?" Daddy Lion asked.

Little Lion didn't want to answer. He kind of turned his head and looked down.

"Little Lion? How was your day at school today? I really want to know. Is there anything wrong?" Daddy Lion asked.

"Well," Little Lion answered, "it started off pretty terrible. Then it just got worse."

"What happened?" asked Daddy Lion.

"I … I …" stuttered Little Lion.

"Come on," coaxed Daddy Lion.

"Well, I … I … I failed my spelling test today. I missed a whole lot of words. When the teacher gave me my test paper, I was so SAD. I didn't want to fail, Daddy Lion. I really didn't," sobbed Little Lion.

"Calm down now. Tell me what happened. Tell me everything," said Daddy Lion.

"Nothing really happened. I just got my test back and saw that I missed almost all my words. And even worse than that, Lisa Lion, who sits beside me, made 100%. Then I was not only SAD, but so JEALOUS of her. I was so FRUSTRATED that I felt like growling at Lisa and maybe giving her a scratch or two," wailed Little Lion.

"Now calm down, Little Lion. Tell me what happened next," said Daddy Lion.

"What happened next? Well, the teacher noticed that I was upset and said that she wanted to talk with me at recess."

"Yes, yes," coached Daddy Lion. "Keep going."

"Well, then I was so WORRIED about what the teacher was going to talk with me about that I couldn't concentrate."

"Then," continued Little Lion, "when recess came, the teacher called me up to her desk and said she thought I was very smart. That

CONFUSED me, because she knew I had failed my spelling test. She said she thought I would do better next time if I studied more. Then I felt GUILTY because, Daddy, I really did not study this week. I have been playing the video games I got for my birthday."

Little Lion hung his head in shame and peeked up to see what Daddy Lion was doing. To his surprise, Daddy Lion was smiling! Little Lion couldn't believe it. "Daddy, aren't you mad at me? Aren't I going to be grounded?"

Daddy Lion just looked at Little Lion and said, "Little Lion, you have had a lot of unwanted feelings today, haven't you?"

"I sure have," answered Little Lion.

"Tell me the feelings that you had during the day that you do not want to have anymore," said Daddy Lion.

"I don't want *any* of the feelings I had today. Not one of them! I don't want to feel *sad, jealous, frustrated, worried, confused,* or *guilty.*"

"I agree. All those feelings are feelings that everyone has sometime or another, but that no one would want to keep. I think I can help you with this," Daddy Lion said confidently.

"Let's see," Daddy Lion continued. "First, you felt sad that you failed your test, right? OK, would you feel better if you made a plan to only play with your video games after you have studied? If you do that, you will have a better chance to do better on your next test. Right?"

Reader: Pause. Ask the children the following question, then continue reading the story.

How do you think Little Lion would feel if he did decide to not play video games until he finished studying? (He would feel happy because he would do better on his tests.)

Little Lion thought for a second, then agreed that this would be a great plan. This plan made Little Lion feel GLAD instead of *sad*. He decided to feel *glad* because he knew he would study and do better on the next test.

"Now, the next feelings you had were *jealousy* and *frustration* because Lisa Lion did better than you on the test. OK, let's think about how to change these feelings. Who was cheering for you the loudest when you won the running race last week?" asked Daddy Lion.

Little Lion hung his head when he remembered Lisa Lion jumping and screaming for him when he crossed the finish line first. "Lisa Lion? I think she cheered the loudest for me."

"I think you are right about that. I never knew a little lion could scream that loudly. Since Lisa is happy for you when you do well on something, do you think you could be happy for her when she does well on something?" Daddy Lion asked wisely.

Reader: Pause. Ask the children the following questions, then continue reading the story.

Do you think Little Lion would feel better if he chose to be happy for Lisa Lion? (Yes.)

Why? (Because feeling happy would feel better than feeling jealous.)

Little Lion knew what his father meant and nodded his head in agreement. Lisa Lion had been his friend for as long as he could remember. He *did* want Lisa to do well. "I am going to decide to feel HAPPY for Lisa instead of *jealous* and *frustrated* because she did well."

"Good for you, son!" said Daddy Lion.

"I believe the next feelings you had were *worry, confusion,* and *guilt.* Let's think about them. Why do you think your teacher called you up at recess to talk with you?" asked Daddy Lion.

Little Lion shrugged his shoulders.

Reader: Pause. Ask the children the following question, then continue reading the story.

Why do you think Little Lion's teacher called him up at recess? (She called him up because she cared about Little Lion and was concerned.)

"I think she called you up because she cares about you. She knows you are smart and was concerned that you had not done your best. I think you could be thankful that you have such a caring teacher. What do you think?" asked Daddy Lion.

"Thankful?" thought Little Lion. But then he remembered how nicely his teacher had spoken. Why, he was lucky to have a teacher that cared about him. "I am going to decide to be THANKFUL for my teacher instead of being *worried, confused,* and *guilty*," Little Lion said proudly.

"That is great!" responded Daddy Lion. "It is critical to choose good feelings whenever possible, and I am proud of you for deciding to choose good feelings. I think that you will feel better for the rest of the day now."

"I sure do," said Little Lion. But then he asked curiously, "Why didn't you get *angry* with me about my failed spelling test?"

"I didn't get *angry* because I chose to be *proud* of you for telling me the truth instead of being *angry* with you about your test score. Besides, I had a few bad test scores in my day and I remember how I felt. I imagined you felt as badly as I did when I got mine," Daddy Lion explained.

This made Little Lion feel TICKLED, because he hadn't known his daddy could do anything bad. Little Lion smiled as his daddy gave him a *proud* hug.

Do you think Little Lion will make the critical decision to choose good feelings from now on? (Yes.)

Why? (Because choosing good feelings whenever possible keeps him happier.)

"Thank you, Daddy, for teaching me how to choose good feelings," said Little Lion.

"Your welcome, son. Now shouldn't you start studying for this week's spelling test?" asked Daddy Lion.

"Yes, sir!" replied Little Lion as he marched to his bedroom to study.

THE CRITICAL DECISION TO
NOT USE DRUGS

Lesson Plan Objectives:

1. Read the story to the children for the purpose of teaching them about the importance of making the critical decision to not use drugs.

2. Discuss the questions before or after reading the story to encourage thinking/talking about the results of choosing to be drug free.

3. Select one or more follow-up activities to give children practical experiences in deciding to not use drugs.

 **LESSON**

Introduction:

▸   Materials needed: Chalkboard and chalk, two packages of drink mix (already sweetened), clear pitchers of water, clear container of dirt, and large stirring spoon for the leader. Paper cup for each child.

▸   Tell the children you have a great surprise for them. Then show them the pitcher of water and the drink mix.

▸   Mix the drink mix and give one empty cup to each child.

▸   After passing out the cups, say:

    Oops! I forgot to add a special ingredient to the drink.

▸   Take out the clear container of dirt and pour the dirt into the drink mix. Stir the dirt into the drink mix and ask:

    Would anyone like to drink this drink mix with dirt?

▶ When the children respond "*No*," ask:

> *Why not?* (Because the dirt messed up the drink mix and dirt would not be good to put into our bodies.)

▶ Then say:

> *That is correct. Just like you know dirt in the drink mix is not good to put into your bodies, it is also not good to put drugs into your bodies. Whatever goes into your body will either help it or hurt it.*

▶ Make a fresh batch of drink mix that does not have anything in it that would be harmful to their bodies and give each child some in his/her cup. (Note: Be sure the children are allowed sugar in their diets. If a child can not have sugar or any other ingredient in the drink mix, give him/her a glass of water.)

▶ While the children are drinking, have them discuss what is good and not good to put into their bodies. Write the students' ideas on the chalkboard.

<u>NOT GOOD</u>

Drugs are not good.
Too much candy is not good.
Dirt is not good.

<u>GOOD</u>

Vegetables are good.
Fruit is good.
Dairy products are good.

▶ Then ask:

> *Would you say that what you put into your bodies is an important decision?* (Yes.)
>
> *Why?* (If you do not make the right decision, you could put things into your body that will hurt it.)

▶ Then say:

> *Another word for important is critical. Because of what we have talked about, we can say that deciding what to put into our bodies is a critical decision.*

Story:

▶ Introduce the story by saying:

Today you are going to hear a story about a boy who makes the critical decision to not use drugs. If you listen closely to this story, it can help you to decide to say "No" to drugs.

▶ Read *Drugs Are Not Cool* (pages 148-152).

Discussion Questions:

▶ Present the following questions to the children. Remind them of the importance of the critical decision to say *"No"* to drugs.

1. *Can drugs ever be good for you?* (Drugs/medicines prescribed by a doctor or bought for you by your family are good for you because they will help you feel better.)

2. *What kinds of drugs are bad for you?* (Any drugs that are not prescribed for you by a doctor or are not bought for you by your family could harm your body. You should take only drugs a doctor prescribes for you or your family buys for you in order to help you feel better.)

3. *What should you say if someone asks you to take drugs that you know are not from your doctor or your family?* (You should say, *"No"* because you have decided to not use drugs.)

4. *Are there different ways to say "No" to someone who is trying to get you to take drugs?* (Yes.)

   Name some ways to say "No" to drugs.

   If not suggested by the children, give the following examples of ways to say "no" to drugs.

   • *You could just say, "No" or say, "No, I don't use drugs."*

- *You could repeat the same sentence over and over if the person keeps asking. "No, I don't use drugs. Again … "No, I don't use drugs." Repeat it as long as the person keeps asking.*

- *You could give an excuse or reason. "No, I don't use drugs. I am hoping I can make the soccer team, so I want my body to be in good shape."*

- *You could change the subject. "No, I don't use drugs. Hey, did you see the ballgame last night on TV?"*

- *You could walk away and not say anything at all.*

- *You could walk away and tell a grown-up.*

- *You could blame someone else for your decision. "No, I don't use drugs. My dad/mom takes me to the doctor once a month to make sure I am drug-free," or "My dad/mom really keeps a close eye on me and I would be grounded forever if I used drugs," or "One of my relatives used drugs and it really messed him/her up bad. I am choosing to stay away from drugs since I have seen what they can do to a person."*

Then say:

Find some way of saying "No" that you are comfortable with and continue to stay drug-free.

Continue the discussion questions by asking:

5. *How can drugs harm your body?* (Different drugs harm the body in different ways. For example: Cigarettes harm your heart and your lungs while alcohol harms your liver and ability to think. Any kind of drug that you are not supposed to take harms your body in some way.)

6. *Why do people use drugs?* (There is no good reason to use drugs, but people sometimes say they use drugs to look cool to a group of people, to fit in with a particular group of people, to appear older than

they really are, to keep people from teasing them, or to try to forget problems they may be having. But actually, drugs only make their problems worse.)

Follow-Up Activities:

ACTIVITY #1

▶ This activity will help reinforce the importance of making the critical decision to not use drugs.

▶ Materials needed: Art paper and crayons for each child.

▶ Distribute art paper and crayons to each child. Then say:

Suppose a rich relative called and said he was going to buy you one car and only one. This relative also said he would let you pick out any car you wanted. What kind of car would you pick for your rich relative to buy you?

▶ Have the children draw pictures of the car they would want. When everyone has finished, allow each child to show his/her picture and describe the car he/she chose.

▶ Then ask:

1. *After you got this car, would you take a hammer and beat some dents into it?* (No.)

2. *After you got this car, would you scribble all over it with a permanent marker?* (No.)

3. *What about taking a screwdriver and scratching marks all over it? Would you do this after you got the car?* (No.)

4. *Why wouldn't you do these things to your car?* (Because I am proud of this car and want to take care of it. It is the only car that my rich relative will buy me, so I want it to continue to run well, look good, and last a long, long time.)

▸ Explain to the class:

Just like you wanted your car to last for a long time, you have just one body that will have to last a long time, in fact, as long as you live.

▸ Then ask:

1. *If you would care enough to take care of a fancy car so it would run well, look good, and last a long time, shouldn't you care enough to take care of your own body so it will work well, look good, and last a long time?* (Yes.)

2. *Will using drugs help your body work well, look good, and last a long time?* (No.)

3. *Why?* (Using drugs will harm our bodies and cause them to not work well, look good, or last a long time.)

ACTIVITY #2

▸ This activity will give the children another source to support the critical decision to not use drugs. The guest speaker can even let the children know the consequences of choosing *to do* drugs.

▸ Materials needed: None

▸ Invite a police office or doctor to speak to your class about the dangers of using drugs.

ACTIVITY #3

▸ This activity will give the children practice in sticking with their critical decision to not use drugs by allowing them time to practice what they could say if/when someone tries to get them to use drugs.

▸ Materials needed: None

▸ Look back at *Discussion Question #4.* Have the children act out different ways they can think of to say "*No*" to someone/a group trying to get them to take drugs. After a while, allow the children to think of some new ways to say "*No*." Allow them to role-play their own ideas.

▸ Conclude the activity by asking each child which way of saying "*No*" would be most comfortable for him/her to use if he/she were ever approached by someone offering drugs.

DRUGS ARE NOT COOL

"Mom," said Tommy as he came into the kitchen from playing outside, "Brian, who lives down the road, smokes cigarettes."

"I know," said Tommy's mother. "He shouldn't smoke, because smoking is bad for his body. I hope he learns better and will quit. Sit down. You look like you are as hot as can be. You must have been playing hard outside."

"I have been," said Tommy.

"Well, I'll fix you something to drink. It will help you cool down. Have a seat at the table," said Tommy's mom.

"Brian really *does* smoke, Mom," Tommy said again.

Seeing that Tommy was curious about Brian's smoking, his mother replied, "Yes, I know. What do you think about that?"

"Honestly, Mom? I think he looks pretty cool. I think smoking makes him look like he is older and tough. I wish I could smoke, too."

Reader: Pause. Ask the children the following questions, then continue reading the story.

Do you think it is cool to smoke? (No.)

Why? (Because cigarettes harm our bodies and there is nothing cool about that.)

"Tommy, did you know that smoking, or using any kind of drug that a doctor does not prescribe for you, will hurt your body. That certainly is not cool," responded his mother. "I truly hope you never decide to put anything into your body that will hurt you."

"But Mom, Brian seems OK when he smokes," said Tommy.

"He may *seem* OK, but the drugs inside a cigarette are harming his body on the inside. This damage could make him very sick. It could even cause him to not be able to do fun activities like running and swimming because the inside of his body will be really messed up," said Tommy's mom.

"I don't know about all this stuff, Mom. I hear people say that drugs are bad, but I really don't understand," said Tommy.

Tommy's mother tried to help him see what she was saying, "It is hard to understand everything, but all you have to know is that whatever you put into your body will either help or hurt your body."

Reader: Pause. Ask the children the following questions, then continue reading the story.

What can you put into your body that is good for you? (Fruits, vegetables, dairy products, etc.)

What can you put into your body that is bad for you? (Drugs.)

Mother continued to explain, "Fruits and vegetables are good for you. Medicine taken like a doctor says it should be taken is good for you. But drugs like cigarettes and alcohol are *not* good for your body. You have to be careful what you put into your body."

"Is my drink ready yet?" asked Tommy.

"Almost," answered Mom. "I am still working on it."

Mom poured a tall glass of Tommy's favorite drink and put several ice cubes into it.

"That sure looks good," said Tommy.

Then Tommy's mother asked, "Tommy, would you please hand me that little potted plant on the counter and a spoon from the drawer?"

"Sure," said Tommy, "but why?"

"I just need your help for a minute. I want to add something to your drink. Then it will be ready," said his mother.

"OK," said Tommy. "What do you want me to do?"

"Well," said Mom, "I would like you to stir your drink after I add a few spoonfuls of dirt from this potted plant."

"*What*?" asked Tommy in disbelief as his mother dumped two huge spoonfuls of dirt into glass.

CRITICAL DECISIONS © 2006 MAR✶CO PRODUCTS, INC. 1-800-448-2197

"Stir that around, then drink up," said Tommy's mom.

Reader: Pause. Ask the children the following questions, then continue reading the story.

Do you think Tommy will drink the drink his mother has made? (No.)

Why? (Because he knows it would not be good for him to drink something that has dirt in it.)

"I'm not going to drink that now," said Tommy. "That's awful!"

"Why do you think that?" asked his mother.

"The dirt messed up my drink and I sure don't want to drink it now," exclaimed Tommy.

"You know what, Tommy? You are right. The dirt messed up the drink. If you were to drink it, you might get sick," said his mother.

"Why do you think I did this? Can you learn a lesson from this?" asked his mother.

Tommy began to see his mom's point.

Reader: Pause. Ask the children the following questions, then continue reading the story.

Do you think Tommy will make the critical decision to not use drugs? (Yes.)

Why? (He has learned a lesson from his mom about how bad it is to put drugs or anything that would hurt him into his body.)

"I guess I understand now," he said. "Drugs are like the dirt. If you put drugs into your body, it will not be good for you. If I know not to drink my favorite drink with dirt in it, I should know not to put other things that will hurt me into my body."

"That's right," said his mom. "You have learned a good lesson. Your body deserves to have good things in it, not things that will hurt you. I'm glad we had this talk. I hope you will remember this lesson and always make the critical decision not to put anything into your body that will do you harm. I want you to learn that a drink with dirt in it is not cool, just like drugs in your body are not cool."

"OK, Mom, you made a good point. I have learned a lesson," said Tommy. "I am going to make the critical decision to never use drugs. Thanks, Mom."

"You're welcome," said Tommy's mom as she poured the drink into the sink. "Now lets start again. OK?"

"OK," said Tommy. And this time, they fixed their drink just right.

THE CRITICAL DECISION TO
TREAT EVERYONE EQUALLY

Lesson Plan Objectives:

1. Read the story to the children for the purpose of teaching them about the importance of making the critical decision to treat everyone equally.

2. Discuss the questions before or after reading the story to encourage thinking/talking about the results of choosing to treat everyone equally.

3. Select one or more follow-up activities to give children practical experiences in treating everyone equally.

 **LESSON**

Introduction:

▶ Materials needed: Two pictures of a rainbow. (One colored with only one color and the other colored with all the colors of a rainbow.)

▶ Show the children the picture of the rainbow that has only one color. Then ask:

What is wrong with this picture? (A rainbow is supposed to be all different colors. A rainbow colored with one color does not look good.)

▶ Show the children the picture of the rainbow with many colors. Then ask:

Which picture is better? (The picture of the rainbow that has many colors is better.)

Why? (It is better because all the colors make the picture prettier.)

▶ Continue the lesson by saying:

The rainbow picture with many different colors was the one you liked better. You liked it because it had many differences. This is very much like real life. If everyone were the same, like the one-color rainbow picture, life would not be as interesting.

Differences make our lives more interesting. Some people do not like differences. They make fun of or will not play with anyone who is different than they are. I hope you don't think that way. I hope you will make the important or critical decision to treat everyone equally.

Story:

▶ Introduce the story by saying:

Today you are going to hear a story about a bouquet of flowers that learn that all their different colors, sizes, and shapes are what makes them so pretty. Once the flowers learn this lesson, they make the critical decision to treat each other equally. Listen closely to the story and you will learn how important it is to decide to treat each person equally.

▶ Read *Flower Power* (pages 158-162).

Discussion Questions:

▶ Present the following questions to the children. Remind them of the importance of the critical decision to treat everyone equally.

1. *Would it be fair for your school to only let green-eyed children have recess?* (No.)

   Why? (It would not be fair because the brown- and blue-eyed children would be left out.)

2. *Would it be fair for your teacher to always let the tallest children line up first?* (No.)

Why? (It would not be fair because the shorter children would feel bad if they always had to line up after the tall children.)

3. *Can you decide how you should feel about or treat someone based on how he or she looks?* (No.)

    Why? (How someone looks is not an indication of what kind of person he/she is. How someone looks should not have anything to do with how you feel about or treat that person.)

4. *How can you decide how you should feel about or treat someone?* (You can decide how you should feel about or treat someone based on how that person acts. For example: If someone is kind and thoughtful, you could decide to feel good about him/her and treat that person nicely. But if someone is hateful and rude, you could feel bad about him/her and treat that person with caution because you would not want to be hurt by him/her.)

5. *What does it mean to treat others the way you want to be treated?* (It means that you want others to decide to treat you nicely, no matter what you look like. So you should treat others nicely, no matter what *they* look like.)

Follow-Up Activities:

ACTIVITY #1

▸   This activity will help the children see that differences in others are acceptable and even beautiful. It will help them see that the critical decision to treat others equally is the right decision to make.

▸   Materials needed: Bulletin board, camera, construction paper, markers, staples, and gluestick for the leader. Scissors for each child.

▸   Using a camera, take a picture of each child's face. Glue the picture to a piece of construction paper larger than the picture. With a permanent marker, draw the shape of a flower around the picture of each child.

▶ Distribute each picture to its owner. Give each child a pair of scissors. Then have the children cut along the drawing of the flower so that the pictures will be in a shape of a flower with the child's face in the center. (Note: Younger children will need help with cutting out the flower shapes.)

▶ Staple the flower-shaped pictures onto a bulletin board so they will look like a pretty bouquet of flowers. Draw stems for the flowers on the bulletin board. Label the bulletin board: *Children are like a bouquet of flowers— beautiful.* (Note: The pictures could also be glued/taped on posterboard and displayed in the hallway.)

▶ Explain to the children:

> *People are just like flowers. Each has a different size, shape, and color. It is these beautiful differences in people that help make our world a more interesting and fun place to live.*

ACTIVITY #2

▶ This activity will reinforce the idea that different colors everywhere are acceptable and beautiful. This will help the children understand that no matter what color eyes, hair, or skin someone has, everyone should be treated equally.

▶ Materials needed: Art paper and crayons for each child.

▶ Distribute a piece of art paper and crayons to each child. Tell the children they may draw anything they like, but they may use only one color. Set a time limit for completion of this activity.

▶ Distribute a second piece of art paper to each child. Tell the children to draw the same picture using as many different colors as they like. Set a time limit for completion of this activity.

▶ Have the children compare the two pictures they have drawn and discuss how using many different colors makes a more beautiful picture.

(Note: This could be a good lesson to display in the hallway. The multicolored pictures could be displayed next to the one-color pictures to show the contrast between dull and pretty. Above the pictures could be the title: *It's Nice To Live In A World That Has Lots Of Pretty Colors To Enjoy.*)

ACTIVITY #3

▸   This activity will remind the children not to judge people according to their looks. It will remind children that what is important is how a person acts.

▸   Materials needed: None

▸   Teach this song to the children to the tune of *"Yankee Doodle."*

Different colors, different shapes,
Different sizes, to-oo.
Being different is OK.
Please know that this is tr-ue.

You don't have to look like her,
Or him or even me-ee.
You're being nice to others is
What everyone should see-ee.

FLOWER POWER

Once upon a time, a beautiful vase of flowers was displayed in a store window. People who walked by saw this beautiful bouquet. There were orange, purple, yellow, blue, and red flowers. There were tall, short, big, and small flowers. Together, they made a wonderful scene. The bouquet of flowers brought joy to everyone who saw it.

Reader: Pause. Ask the children the following question, then continue reading the story.

How do you think these flowers were able to bring people joy? (They were able to bring joy because all the different colors, sizes, and shapes of the flowers were very cheerful to see.)

An elderly lady who was very ill passed by. When she saw the flowers, they looked so pretty that she stopped and smiled. The bouquet felt happy that it was able to help this lady find joy in her day.

Another time, a child who was crying walked by with his mother. When the child saw the vase of flowers, he wiped away his tears and had a more peaceful look on his face. These, and many other incidents like them, made the flowers feel very happy and proud.

One morning, the flowers began talking about how happy they were that they could bring joy to others. The orange flowers spoke up first and said, "Did you all see how that older lady looked happier when she noticed how tall and beautiful we orange flowers are? We feel proud that we made her day better."

The blue flowers spoke up next, "Hey, wait a minute! We're sure that it was *us* that the lady was looking at and that we blue flowers made the little boy feel better, too."

"We beg to differ with you both," said the big, puffy red flowers. "We think it was us who caused all the people passing by to feel happier.

Anyone can see that we are the most cheerful-looking flowers. We are the best flowers in this vase by far."

"No, no! We must speak up at this point!" shouted the yellow flowers. "We are certainly the most cheerfully-colored flowers in this vase. Everyone knows that yellow is the happiest color in the world. Why, we are the color of the sun, and we have a gorgeous shape. Look how perfectly round we are. We are round like the beautiful sun. There is no doubt that we are the best flowers in this vase."

Reader: Pause. Ask the children the following question, then continue reading the story.

Is one of the groups of flowers better than the others? (No, all the groups of flowers are equal in their ability to make the bouquet beautiful.)

The flowers continued to argue all day. They argued so much that they were no longer able to be perky and happy. The flowers fussed and fussed so much that they began to look wilted and limp. When people passed by, they saw the bouquet of flowers, but they no longer felt cheerful. In fact, the way the flowers looked now made some people feel *worse* after seeing them.

Before closing the store, the flowers overheard the manager say, "It's time to throw out these flowers. They're looking quite pitiful. Someone get a new arrangement ready tomorrow after we open."

The flowers wilted even more after hearing this and were very quiet. After the store workers left, the tiny purple flowers finally decided to say, "Something is really wrong. Just yesterday, the store manager was bragging about us and the people who passed by were smiling because of us. What are we going to do? We used to make people feel good when they looked at us. And now, in just one day of arguing, we are falling apart and doing no good at all. We must think of something to change. After all, it is not only us that is at stake, it is also people's happiness when they look at us.

Reader: Pause. Ask the children the following question, then continue reading the story.

What must the flowers do to be happy and pretty again? (The flowers must make the critical decision to say they are sorry to one another and decide to treat each other equally instead of saying one group of flowers is better than another.)

CRITICAL DECISIONS © 2006 MAR✱CO PRODUCTS, INC. 1-800-448-2197

The blue flowers spoke up next and said, "We agree that we do need to try to get back to the way we were. Our trouble started with all of us arguing this morning about who was the best. We were even a part of this argument. Right here and now, we want to say we're sorry for our part in this argument." The statement from the blue flowers made the other flowers feel a little better.

Then the red flowers said, "We, too, were a part of this argument. We know now that we hurt a lot of your feelings and we want to say that we are sorry." Hearing this, the flowers felt even better.

The purple flowers spoke up again, "Maybe we are all realizing that all of us were wrong for fussing about who is the best. Our arguing has made each of us feel terrible, and when we feel terrible, we are not able to be the best we all can be." All the flowers agreed.

Finally the orange flowers spoke. "As hard as it is to say, we remember that we started this argument. We want to say we are sorry and we want to thank the purple flowers for showing us what we had done wrong. We were all getting into a mess, and maybe now we can make things better. You have done something special for us by making us realize how wrong we were to think any one of us was better than another. Thanks again, purple flowers."

The yellow flowers agreed wholeheartedly.

At that very moment, all of the flowers physically perked up.

Reader: Pause. Ask the children the following question, then continue reading the story.

Why did the flowers perk up at this point? (They perked up because they had made the critical decision to make each other feel better by realizing that they were all equal in their abilities to make their bouquet beautiful.)

"Wow!' the blue flowers said, looking at the tall orange flowers. "Orange flowers, you certainly do add a happy look to our vase. We appreciate your color and tall size."

At that moment, the flowers began to perk up more.

All the flowers repeated that they were sorry and told each other how each of them was special because of their color, size, and shape.

With each added compliment and each added apology, the flowers became more beautiful and healthier-looking. In fact, they were even more gorgeous than they had been before the argument.

The next day, the store employee came to throw out the flowers. What he saw amazed him! As he looked at the flowers, he said, "These flowers are prettier than ever! I can hardly believe my eyes! They make me feel cheerful just looking at them."

The manager heard this and came over to look. "I certainly agree," he said. "These flowers are wonderful today. I wonder how this could have happened?"

The flowers were overjoyed to hear this. They became even happier when they again saw a smile from someone passing by.

"Boy, we sure learned a good lesson," the orange flowers said. "I'm glad we have now decided that we, together, are *all* important no matter what color, size, or shape we are. As a team, we truly can make our little corner of the world a happier place. We're happy we learned this lesson and glad we made the critical decision to treat each other equally. Now, let's enjoy the day and spread some of our happiness to others who pass our way."

And they did.

 THE CRITICAL DECISION TO
FOLLOW RULES

Lesson Plan Objectives:

1. Read the story to the children for the purpose of teaching them about the importance of making the critical decision to follow rules.

2. Discuss the questions before or after reading the story to encourage thinking/talking about the results of choosing to follow rules.

3. Select one or more follow-up activities to give children practical experiences in following rules.

✺✺✺✺ LESSON ✺✺✺✺

Introduction:

▸   Materials needed: Four dice and chalkboard and chalk or marker board and markers for the leader.

▸   Divide the class into two teams. Call one child from each team to the front of the room and give each child two dice.

▸   Ask the children to roll the dice, then announce who won the round or that it was a tie. (Note: A child wins the round and receives one point by rolling the dice with two hands instead of one. The children do not know this rule. Let them be confused about how to win in order to show them the importance of knowing and following rules.) Record the teams' score on the board. Continue calling up team members, having them roll the dice without knowing the rules, and recording their scores on the board.

▸   After a while ask:

    Do you like this game or is it confusing? (It is confusing.)

    Why? (It is confusing because they don't know how to really play the game. They don't know the rules.)

▶ Then tell the children:

Without rules, the game will not be fun to play and will be very confusing.

Story:

▶ Introduce the story by saying:

Today you are going to hear a story about a kite that learns the importance of rules and makes the critical decision to follow rules. Listen closely to the story and you will learn how important it is to make the critical decision to follow rules.

▶ Read *Rules* (pages 167-173).

Discussion Questions:

▶ Present the following questions to the children. Remind them of the importance of the critical decision to follow rules.

1. *Why do we have rules?* (We have rules to keep us safe and help us have fun.)

2. *What would happen if there were no rules?* (If there were no rules, we would not be safe. It would be hard to have any fun, because there would be so much confusion and disorder.)

3. *What are some rules you have in your school and how do these rules help you?* (a. Don't run in the halls: This helps because if children run, they might fall and get hurt. b. Keep your hands and feet to yourself: This helps because children won't be bothering each other. c. Raise your hand before speaking: This helps because children will be able to take turns speaking. d. Treat others the way you want to be treated: This helps children treat each other nicely. Accept any other appropriate rules.)

4. *What are some rules you have in your home and how are these rules helpful?* (a. Keep your bedroom clean: This helps keep you safe so you won't trip on things and fall. b. Don't jump on the beds: This helps keep you safe because you won't fall and get hurt. c. Brush your teeth: This helps keep you healthy. d. Wash your hands before dinner: This helps keep you healthy. Accept any other appropriate rules.)

5. *What are some rules you have in your community and how are these rules helpful?* (a. Don't speed: This helps keep drivers from having accidents. b. Don't steal from others: This helps you get along better with others and avoid breaking the law. c. Children must go to school: This helps children learn. d. Use crosswalks when crossing the street: This helps people to be safe. Accept any other appropriate rules.)

Follow-Up Activities:

ACTIVITY #1

▶ This activity will help the children see the importance of rules and why it is critical that people make the decision to follow them.

▶ Materials needed: A pair of dice for each group of children.

▶ Divide the children into groups of four or five and give each group two dice.

▶ Ask the children to think of rules for a game using the dice.

▶ Agree on a set of rules and let the children play the game.

▶ After playing the game, allow time for the children to discuss how rules were needed in order for everyone to have fun playing the game.

ACTIVITY #2

▶ This activity will give the children another source to support the critical decision to follow rules.

▶ Materials needed: None

▶ Invite a guest speaker to come to the class and explain the importance of deciding to follow rules. (Guest speakers could be one or more of the following: police officer, firefighter, lifeguard, team coach, principal, guest teacher, parent.)

ACTIVITY #3

▶ This activity will be fun and will help the children remember the importance of having rules and why it is critical for everyone to follow rules.

▶ Materials needed: None

▶ Teach the children the following rap. The verses should be recited in rap style.

Rules are cool.
You know they are.
We need rules
Near and far.

Rrr rules, rule.
Rrr rules, rule.

Rules are needed.
You know it's true.
Rules help me
And rules help you.

Rrr rules, rule.
Rrr rules, rule.

Follow rules
Every day.
You'll have fun.
And no trouble. OK!

Rrr rules, rule.
Rrr rules, rule.

CRITICAL DECISIONS © 2006 MAR*CO PRODUCTS, INC. 1-800-448-2197

 # RULES

Kite couldn't believe it! Someone had picked him up off of the shelf and was going to buy him.

"Wow! This is great!" thought Kite.

Kite heard the lady tell the cashier she was going to give him to her nephew, Kyle, for his birthday.

"Wonderful! I'll belong to a boy! I'll bet we will play together every breezy day. I can't wait to fly!" Kite thought to himself.

At the birthday party, Kite finally felt someone lift him up again and say, "Kyle, here is a present from your Aunt Debbie. Open it up and see what it is."

When Kyle opened Kite up, he loved him right away. Kite knew that because of what Kyle said.

"This is just what I have been wanting! Thanks a lot Aunt Debbie. When can we fly it?" Kyle asked excitedly.

Aunt Debbie told him they would fly the kite as soon as the party was over. Kyle and Kite could hardly wait.

As soon as everyone had left the party, Aunt Debbie asked, "Are you ready to fly your kite?"

"You bet," answered Kyle. "Let's do it!"

"Hold on just a second, please," Aunt Debbie said. "Before we fly the kite, you have to promise to follow some kite-flying rules."

"Rules! Yuck! I don't want to have rules when it comes to doing something fun. Rules take the fun out of everything," complained Kyle.

"Why, Kyle," Aunt Debbie answered, "just the opposite is true. Rules *help* you have fun. They also keep you safe."

Reader: Pause. Ask the children the following questions, then continue reading the story.

Do you agree that rules help you to have fun and help you stay safe? (Yes.)

Can you give me some examples of why this is so? (1. The rule of no running in the hallways at school helps children not fall and get hurt so they can continue having fun learning at school. 2. The rule of sharing/ taking turns helps children have more friends and not get into any arguments. 3. The rule of doing your homework helps children not get into trouble and helps them learn. 4. The rule of looking both ways before crossing the street, helps people be safe so they can continue having fun. 5. The rule of wearing seat belts helps people be safe so they can continue to have a pleasant drive in their cars.)

Kyle looked discouraged, so Aunt Debbie started to explain. "Yes, Kyle, rules are good things to have. For example, grown-ups have rules to not speed in their cars so they can continue on their drive and will not have accidents. Grown-ups also have rules they follow at their work so they will continue to get paid at their jobs and not get fired. Schools have rules to help children continue to have fun learning and not get hurt. Rules are wonderful to have. You will see. These kite rules are good to have."

"OK," said Kyle. "I'll listen."

"That's my boy," said Aunt Debbie with a smile.

Aunt Debbie explained the rules carefully and Kyle and Kite listened.

The rules were:

1. Always fly the kite in open areas, not around electrical wires that could shock you, and not around trees because the kite could get tangled up in the branches.

2. Find which direction the wind is blowing and run into the wind.

3. Pull the kite along behind you until the kite is picked up by the wind.

4. When the kite is in the air, don't let go of the kite string. Keep the kite in your control.

5. Have a great time.

Kyle agreed to the rules. Then Aunt Debbie helped him get his kite in the air for the first time. It was fabulous! Kyle loved flying his kite, and Kite was thrilled that he got to go high into the air. Kite, Kyle, and Aunt Debbie had a wonderful time.

After that day, Kyle would race home any breezy afternoon to fly his kite. Kite loved to be flown and looked forward to when Kyle would come home. Kyle and Kite were both careful to remember the rules Aunt Debbie had told them and, because they remembered and followed the rules, they were able to be safe and have a lot of fun together.

Kyle and Kite got to be very good at flying. Kyle would fly Kite high in the air and let Kite soar in his open front yard as high as the string would allow. Kite could see for miles and loved the way it felt to be so far up in the sky. Kite, with Kyle's knowledge and control, could do flips, turns, dives, and loopty-loops. Kite and Kyle were a great team.

One day, however, Kite began to wonder, "Hmmmmm, if it is this much fun being this high up doing all these tricks, I wonder how much fun it would be to go even higher? I wonder how much fun I could have without Kyle holding onto my string? Why, I could go anywhere I wanted to go. I could do as many tricks as I wanted. Hmmmmm … I'll bet if I were free from Kyle and the rules, I would have more fun than ever. I am going to decide not to follow the rules. I have decided to be completely free."

Reader: Pause. Ask the children the following questions, then continue reading the story.

Do you think Kite would have more fun if he did not follow the rules? (No.)

Why? (Kite could get in terrible messes and not be able to have fun with Kyle any more if he does not follow the rules.)

What might happen? (Kite could get tangled up in electrical wires or tree limbs, could blow far away and get lost from Kyle, or could fall hard on the ground and get broken. Accept any other appropriate answers.)

With this thought of being free from rules, Kite decided to break loose from Kyle's hold. Kite tugged on the string as hard as he could, trying to break loose. Kyle sensed what Kite was trying to do and called out loudly, "Don't break loose from your string. That's against the rules!"

Hearing this, Kite thought, "Kyle just wants to control me and doesn't want me to have my freedom. He and his aunt don't know everything. I know I will love being free from rules and Kyle."

Kite tugged even harder, trying to break loose. Then Kite yelled into the wind, "I don't want to follow your rules any more. I don't want your control. I want to be free to do whatever I want!"

Seeing what was going on and afraid of what would happen, Kyle yelled, "You will be in danger if you don't follow the rules."

But Kite thought that Kyle probably just didn't want him to be free to have his own fun, so he tugged even harder.

Desperate, Kyle tried to remind Kite, "The rules we have are for our protection and to help us have fun."

As Kite began to tug even harder, Kyle remembered what his Aunt Debbie had said when helping him learn to fly his kite. He remembered that she said everyone has rules to follow: rules for driving a car, rules for people's jobs, and rules at school. Kyle wondered why Kite didn't want to follow the kite rules any more.

"Stop tugging so hard," Kyle yelled as he felt Kite pull harder and harder.

But Kite did not listen. He tugged with all his might and finally broke loose from Kyle.

"Ahhh, Yeah!" screamed Kite as he swirled up and up farther into the sky. Kite did whirls and turns and loopty-loops like he had never done before. "This is great! I am higher than I ever dreamed I could go. I love this. I knew I didn't need any old rules," Kite thought excitedly.

But … just as Kite was thinking this, a gust of wind whipped him around and around so fast that he couldn't even see straight.

Then, when he *could* see straight, Kite saw something terrible. "I'm heading *straight* toward those trees. Oh, no! Help!" cried Kite.

But there was no way Kyle could help now. Kite was free and Kyle had no control.

Kyle watched helplessly as Kite dove with a hard crash into the backyard trees.

"Oh, no!" screamed Kyle. "Oh, no!"

Kyle ran to call Aunt Debbie. She came over right away. When she arrived, Kyle showed her what had happened.

"It looks like your kite would not cooperate with the rules that we agreed upon," said Aunt Debbie. She tilted her head to look up into the tree and pretended to talk to the kite. "When you don't follow the rules, Kite, you get yourself into a mess."

CRITICAL DECISIONS © 2006 MAR·CO PRODUCTS, INC. 1-800-448-2197

Kite sighed and thought, "I realize that now."

Reader: Pause. Ask the children the following questions, then continue reading the story.

Do you think Kite will make the critical decision to follow the rules from now on? (Yes.)

Why? (He learned the hard way that rules really do keep you safe and help you to have fun.)

Aunt Debbie got a very tall ladder in hopes of getting Kite down and having him repaired for Kyle.

Kite was tangled, bumped, and bruised. Now, he definitely understood the rules that Aunt Debbie had tried to teach them. Kite knew that the rules had kept him from getting into this kind of trouble before.

Kite thought, "If I had only listened to Aunt Debbie and her rules, I wouldn't be in this terrible fix. Kyle and I could still be having fun."

Aunt Debbie climbed up, up, and up and finally got to where Kite was caught in the tree. She carefully untangled Kite and removed him from the branches. Step by step she brought Kite back down to Kyle.

"How bad is the kite hurt?" asked Kyle, afraid to look.

Aunt Debbie replied, "It's not as bad as it could have been. I think I can repair it and you can fly together again. We'll tie a good knot in the string and, hopefully, the kite won't try to get away any more."

"You don't have to worry about me trying to get away any more," Kite thought. "I have made the critical decision to follow the rules from now on."

After Kite was repaired and the string tied tightly, Kyle and Kite had great fun on every breezy day. They both followed the rules from then on.

THE CRITICAL DECISION TO BE THANKFUL

Lesson Plan Objectives:

1. Read the story to the children for the purpose of teaching them about the importance of making the critical decision to be thankful for what they have.

2. Discuss the questions before or after reading the story to encourage thinking/talking about the results of choosing to be thankful.

3. Select one or more follow-up activities to give children practical experiences in being thankful.

 **LESSON**

Introduction:

▶   Begin by asking the children to name:

- some things they are thankful for (toys, beds, lights, clothes, etc.)

- people they are thankful for (Mom, Dad, guardian, aunt, uncle, teacher, etc.)

- places they are thankful for (home, school, church, gym, park, ballfield, etc.)

- animals they are thankful for (pets, other animals.)

▶   Then continue the lesson by saying:

I am really happy that you have thought of so much to be thankful for. Sometimes people get so busy with what they are doing in their everyday lives, they forget to think of all they have to be thankful for. Recognizing what you have to be thankful for is saying that you believe the people and things you are thankful for are important.

Recalling these things is not automatic. It is something you make a decision to do and it is an important decision. Another word for important is critical *and recognizing what you have to be thankful for is a critical decision.*

Story:

▶ Introduce the story by saying:

Today you are going to hear a story about a girl who makes the critical decision to be thankful for all she has.

▶ Read *Connie Decides To Be Thankful* (pages 180-185).

Discussion Questions:

▶ Present the following questions to the children. Remind them of the importance of the critical decision to be thankful.

1. *Why do people take time to be thankful on Thanksgiving Day?* (People take time to be thankful on Thanksgiving Day in remembrance of the Pilgrims being thankful for the Native Americans' help and for being in America, where they could worship freely. On Thanksgiving Day, people stop and give thanks for America and for all the blessings we have here.)

2. *Can people take time to be thankful any time of the year?* (Yes. People can and should take time to be thankful throughout the whole year.)

3. *Why is it important for people to decide to be thankful for their blessings?* (It is important for people to be thankful for their blessings because they will be happier and realize they have wonderful things going on in their lives.)

4. *When you see someone who is having a hard time finding anything to be thankful for, what should you do?* (With your parents' or teachers' permission, you could try to help that person by being kind to him/her or by trying to help with whatever is making him/her sad.)

5. *What are some things you can do to help others have things to be thankful for?* (With your parents' or teachers' permission, you can take clothes and/or toys to a charity organization that gives these things to those who need them, help a nice neighbor with work he/she has to do, donate money to an organization that helps people in need, visit elderly people in a rest home, etc.)

Follow-Up Activities:

ACTIVITY #1

▸ This activity can teach children that they do have things to be thankful for, but that in order to identify them, they may have to look at situations in a different way.

▸ Materials needed: None

▸ Say to the children:

> Sometimes people do not see that they have anything to be thankful for, but most people do have a lot to be thankful for. For example:

>> A person with a sprained ankle may feel unlucky, but this person could be thankful that he or she is able to read a lot of good books while the leg is healing.

>> A child may feel unlucky because he or she has to be in school on a sunny, warm day, but the child could choose to feel thankful for being able to go to school and learn new things and see his or her friends.

>> A child may feel bad because he or she got into trouble for running in the halls, but he or she could choose to feel thankful that the school has rules to keep everyone safe.

> In most cases, people have a choice of complaining about situation or finding something to be thankful for in the situation.

► Ask the children to think of ways a person could view the following situations in a thankful manner.

   1. *You don't like what your mother fixed for supper.* (Instead of being upset about what is for supper, you could choose to be thankful that you have food to eat.)

   2. *You are upset that you have to take turns with your sister on the sliding board.* (Instead of being upset about this, you could choose to be thankful that you have a sibling to play with.)

   3. *You are mad that your parents make you go to bed early each night when you want to stay up and watch TV.* (Instead of being upset about going to bed early, you could choose to be thankful that your parents love you enough to make you go to bed early so you will feel good the next day.)

ACTIVITY #2

► This activity will teach children that it is nice to say "*Thank you*" to people in their lives for whom they are thankful.

► Materials needed: Paper and pencil for each child. Overhead projector, transparency, and transparency marker or chart paper and marker for the leader (optional).

► Have the children think of someone for whom they are thankful.

► Distribute paper and pencil to each child and have each child write a letter to the person for whom he/she is thankful, telling why he/she is grateful for knowing that person. (Note: Younger children could draw a picture of the person for whom they are thankful.)

► You may want to model the assignment by writing a letter on an overhead projector or chart paper for the children to view. The letter should follow standard letter-writing format:

   Introduction: Say "*Hi*" and that you wanted to write and tell this person how thankful you are for him/her.

Body: Tell the person to whom you are writing one to three things that he/she has done that make you thankful for him/her.

Closing: Say "*Thank you*" for what he/she has done and that you are glad to know him/her.

Signature: Sign your name.

ACTIVITY #3

▸ This activity gives children the opportunity to examine and record different aspects of their lives for which they are thankful.

▸ Materials needed: Copy of *I Am Thankful For ...* (page 179), a pencil, and crayons for each child.

▸ Distribute the activity sheet, pencil, and crayons to each child.

▸ Instruct the children to draw a picture in each square to illustrate each title.

▸ When everyone has finished, have the children share their pictures with the class.

▸ The completed pictures could be displayed on a bulletin board with the title: *Our Class Is Very Thankful.*

Name _____

I AM THANKFUL FOR ...

A Person I Am Thankful For ...

An Animal I Am Thankful For ...

A Place I Am Thankful For ...

A Thing I Am Thankful For ...

CONNIE DECIDES TO BE THANKFUL

"Wake up, Connie! It's time to get ready. Our relatives will be here soon to have Thanksgiving dinner with us. I need you to get dressed and help me by setting the table and getting some of the board games from the hall closet for us to play after dinner," called Connie's mom.

"Awww, Mom, I don't want to get up. Just five more minutes … " complained Connie.

"You heard me, Connie! Now get up and get dressed. I need your help," Mom insisted.

Connie got up from bed and slowly went to her closet. As she peered into her closetful of clothes, she said, "Awww, I hate all my clothes. I don't have anything that looks like what kids my age are wearing."

Connie pushed aside outfit after outfit, searching for something she might want to wear.

Disgusted and angry, Connie yelled downstairs to her mom, "I need to go shopping today instead of staying here for Thanksgiving dinner. I don't have any decent clothes."

"You have more than enough clothes," Mom yelled back. "Now hurry up and get dressed. Bring the games when you come down. I have the dishes and silverware out for you to put around on the table."

Connie slipped on the next outfit in line in her closet rack, then looked in her mirror. "I hate this outfit," she said aloud.

CRITICAL DECISIONS © 2006 MAR*CO PRODUCTS, INC. 1-800-448-2197

Then she went to the hall closet. She looked over the many games to choose from, but nothing suited her. "All these games are boring. People ought to change the spelling of *board games* to *bored games*, because you get bored when you play them," she grumbled.

Without caring which games she took, Connie picked a few of the boxes and went downstairs.

"Here are the boring board games, Mom," said Connie.

"Fine," replied her mother as she went on peeling potatoes. "Put them in the living room and then set the table, please."

Connie put the board games on the living room coffee table. Then she went into the dining room and started placing the dishes and silverware around the table.

"Don't forget that the napkins go under the forks to the left of the plates and the knives and spoons go to the right of the plates," her mother called from the kitchen.

"I know, I know," said Connie under her breath. Then Connie continued to mumble, "I dread Thanksgiving dinner. We have to eat all kinds of food that is good for us. I wish we could just have soda and chips or something tasty like that."

"What are you saying?" asked Mother.

"Nothing, Mom, nothing," replied Connie.

After the table was set, Connie went back to her bedroom, flopped onto her bed, and said, "I wish I could just stay in here and not be a part of anything that has to do with Thanksgiving this year."

Reader: Pause. Ask the children the following questions, then continue reading the story.

Do you think Connie has things to be thankful for? (Yes.)

What? (She has food, her family, and clothes.)

Why isn't Connie thankful? (She has a poor attitude and does not see all her blessings.)

Then Connie reached for her remote control and turned on her TV. "I'll just lie here and watch TV. Maybe Mom will leave me alone for a while."

Connie turned on the TV and lay back on her pillows to watch.

"Oh, that's just great," said Connie sarcastically as she looked at the screen. "The boring news. I'm changing the channel."

Connie pushed the remote to change the channel, but the remote would not work. She got up and tried to manually change the channel, but that did not work, either. The TV simply would not change stations.

"Stupid TV!" yelled Connie. "Fine! I'll just watch whatever!"

An announcer on a local news station was talking. He said, "Heartbreaking news here in Drakesboro. The Williams family lost its home last night in a three-alarm fire. Although they were not able to save anything inside the house, the family stated they would still be grateful this Thanksgiving because everyone in the house got out safely."

Connie looked at the pictures of the burned-out house and gasped. Then the announcer continued to speak, "A financial fund has been set up to help this family. If you would like to help the Williams family, call the number you see on the screen."

"Oh, my!" cried Connie out loud. "The Williams family? That's Lori's family. Lori goes to my school. She is a couple of years younger than I am, but I see her at our home ballgames. She always helps her parents at the concession stand. I'm glad she and her family are all right."

Then Connie thought more about her situation compared with theirs. "Oh, I feel so sorry for them! All their belongings—clothes, games, food. Everything that I have, they don't have. It's all gone."

Reader: Pause. Ask the children the following question, then continue reading the story.

What lesson do you think Connie will learn from the news report? (She will learn that she has been ungrateful for all she has. She will learn to be more thankful and may decide to help the Williams family.)

All of a sudden, Connie felt very, very guilty. She thought to herself, "I have complained about all the things I have. I should have been grateful for all that I have. I am really ashamed of myself."

Then, Connie focused on the television report. They were showing a picture of the Williams house again. Nothing was left. When they showed the telephone number on the screen for people who wanted to help, Connie reached for a pencil and pad of paper and wrote down the number. Then she raced downstairs.

When Connie reached the bottom of the stairs, she saw her mother putting butter on the rolls for dinner.

Connie ran over to her mother and gave her a big hug. Then she said, "Thanks, Mom for fixing such a good Thanksgiving dinner and for all you do for me. I am very thankful for everything I have this Thanksgiving Day. I love you so much!"

 CRITICAL DECISIONS © 2006 MAR∗CO PRODUCTS, INC. 1-800-448-2197

Connie's mother was surprised at how happy Connie had become and asked, "Well, Connie, what has brought about this thankful and cheerful attitude? You certainly have changed from the way you were feeling when you woke up this morning."

Connie told her mother about the news report on the Williams family and how it had taught her to be thankful for all she had. She showed her mother the phone number that she had copied down. Then she said, "Since I have so much, Mom, I want to give the babysitting money I earned last month to the Williams fund-raiser."

Reader: Pause. Ask the children the following question, then continue reading the story.

How do you think Connie's mother will feel about Connie's request to help this needy family? (She will feel proud of her daughter because Connie has decided to be thankful for what she has and is willing to share part of her good fortune with others.)

Connie's mother looked into her daughter's eyes and could tell that Connie truly had made a critical decision to be thankful and to help others. She was very proud of Connie's decisions and said, "I think that would be a wonderful act of kindness. Connie, I am so proud of you!"

Mother added, "Connie, your enthusiasm for helping is very touching. I am proud of you for wanting to give your money to help this family. Let's call the number right now. I would like to give to this family as well. We have much to be thankful for, and it is right to help others in need."

As she gave her mom the number to call, Connie knew this would be a Thanksgiving to remember for years to come, because it was this Thanksgiving Day that she made the critical decision to be thankful for all her blessings.

Connie's mother dialed the number and both she and Connie felt true happiness as they pledged their donation. It was a great Thanksgiving Day!

THE CRITICAL DECISION TO
CARE FOR YOUR PETS

Lesson Plan Objectives:

1. Read the story to the children for the purpose of teaching them about the importance of making the critical decision to care for their pets.

2. Discuss the questions before or after reading the story to encourage thinking/talking about the results of choosing to care for pets.

3. Select one or more follow-up activities to give children practical experience in caring for pets.

 LESSON

Introduction:

▸ Materials needed: Copy of *My Pet* (page 196), a pencil, and crayons or markers for each child.

▸ Distribute *My Pet*, a pencil, and crayons or markers to each child. Review the directions and have the children complete the activity sheet. When the children have completed the activity sheet, allow them to share their work.

Story:

▸ Introduce the story by saying:

> *Taking care of pets is critical. That means it is very important. It is also a decision that you must make. You may decide not to take care of your pet and hope someone else will do it. That is not a good idea because a pet that is not taken care of could get sick and die. Or you may decide to take care of your pet. Whether or not to take care of your pet is a critical decision that you must make.*

Today you are going to hear a story about a girl who makes the critical decision to care for her pets. If you listen closely to the story, you will learn all the things a pet needs.

▸ Read *Becky's Valentine Friends* (pages 191-195).

Discussion Questions:

▸ Present the following questions to the children. Remind them of the importance of the critical decision to care for their pets.

1. *What are some nice things pets can do for you?* (Pets can be good company, cheer you up by just being with you, make you happy by playing with you, and help keep you safe by barking to let you know someone is at your house or on your property.)

2. *What are some nice things you can do for your pets?* (You can make sure your pets are well taken care of by giving them baths, clean shelter from bad or extreme weather, fresh water and food, taking them to a vet when needed, and giving them love.)

3. *Why do animals need us to care for them?* (Pets depend on us to care for them because they can't go to the grocery store to get their food, build their own houses, get good exercise if they are on a chain, clean up their messes from being in a pen, give themselves baths, or drive themselves to the vet. Pets do nice things for their owners, and owners should, in return, take good care of them. Pets depend on us for many things.)

4. *Do animals have feelings?* (Yes. Animals can feel happy when they are loved, mad if someone is mean to them, scared of storms, sad if they are in a dirty pen, bored if they are always on a chain and not played with, hungry/thirsty when they do not have food or water, proud when they do tricks that please you, sleepy when they do not have good sleep, and silly so they do crazy things sometimes.)

5.   *If someone were thinking about getting a pet for the first time, what advice would you give him or her?* (You could tell this person that a pet can be good company and a lot of fun, but a pet needs the kind of care listed in the answers to Discussion Question #2.)

To expand on the topic, you may ask the following questions. Provide additional information as required.

6.   *What are some things that people must do to care for animals that are not pets?* (People need to follow hunting rules so that not too many animals are killed; be careful not to pollute, because too much pollution harms the animals; and be careful about cutting down too many trees, because without forests many animals will have nowhere to live.)

7.   *What are some things you can do to cut down on the chance of being bitten by a dog?* (According to the Dog Bite Prevention Campaign, you should not run past a dog because dogs naturally love to chase and catch things. Never disturb a dog that's caring for puppies, sleeping, or eating. If threatened by a dog, do not scream, but speak calmly and firmly. Avoid eye contact and stay where you are until the dog leaves or back away slowly until the dog is out of sight. Do not turn and run. If you fall or are knocked to the ground, curl into a ball. Put your hands over your head and neck to protect your face.)

(Note: Reinforce the information on avoiding being bitten by a dog by having the children role-play not disturbing a sleeping or eating dog and not disturbing a female dog feeding her puppies.)

Follow-Up Activities:

ACTIVITY #1

▸   This activity will teach children how to properly pet their pets. (Remind the children never to pet an animal that they do not know well.)

▸   Materials needed: Furry rug and footstool or chair for the leader.

▶ Place a furry rug on a footstool or chair. Pat and rub the furry rug to demonstrate how a person should pet a pet.

▶ Show the children that you are not being rough or pulling the pet's hair, but are being gentle and kind.

▶ Allow each child to come up and pet the rug in the manner you demonstrated.

ACTIVITY #2

▶ This activity will give the children another source who will support the critical decision to care for their pets.

▶ Materials needed: None

▶ Invite a humane shelter worker to come to your class to discuss how the shelter cares for animals.

ACTIVITY #3

▶ This activity combines helping homeless animals and a service learning project.

▶ Materials needed: Camera for the leader. Donations of money from the children.

▶ Have a fund-raiser for the humane shelter in your community.

▶ Your theme could be: "*No Sleep Until We Help The Animals.*"

▶ With this theme in mind, you could have every child bring a dollar (or whatever amount he/she can bring) and wear his/her pajamas to school to show support for the homeless animals in your community. After collecting and counting the money that morning, you could take your class's picture. Sending the picture and a small write-up to the local newspaper would be a good way to show the community that your class is doing its part to make a positive difference in this world/community.

ACTIVITY #4

▶ This activity will instill pride in the children because of their critical decision to care for their pets.

▶ Materials needed: Bulletin board, photographs of children's pets, and newspaper article from Activity #3 (optional).

▶ Ask the children to bring in photographs of their pets to share with the class.

▶ Make a bulletin board composed of the children's pet pictures, the activity sheet completed in the *Introduction* of this lesson, and the newspaper article (if available).

ACTIVITY #5

▶ This activity will motivate the children to make the critical decision to care for their pets. (Note: Prior to presenting this activity, be sure no one in the class/group is allergic to animals.)

▶ Materials needed: Children's pets

▶ Ask the parents of some of the children to bring their pets to school to show the class.

▶ Be sure to verify that the pets that will be brought pose NO threat and will be on a leash or in a cage while they visit your class.

BECKY'S VALENTINE FRIENDS

"I'm sorry you're sick, Becky. I know today is your class's Valentine party, but you are still running a temperature. It would not be wise for you to go to school today," said Becky's mom. "I'm sure you will be better in another day or two. Ms. Allison said she would collect your Valentine cards and have them ready for me to pick up after school today."

Becky nodded to her mom, then rolled over without saying another word. She had looked forward to this party for days. She had made her Valentine Box at school by covering it with aluminum foil and taping red hearts all over it. It really looked beautiful. She had also made Valentines for everyone. She was so disappointed about her fever. She really felt okay after her mother gave her the medicine from the doctor, but she was still very tired most of the time.

Becky's mind drifted to the classroom. She thought, "I bet everyone is smiling and looking forward to eating cake and cookies. I bet everyone is anxious to open their Valentines, too. I bet my class is having fun right now, and I bet they are all laughing and giggling together. I bet everyone is being nice to each other and everyone is happy. But I'm not happy. I am here by myself. I am not happy at all. I am not having any fun, either! I am lonely and sad on this Valentine's Day, and it's awful. I hate it that I can't spend Valentine's Day with my friends."

Becky's dogs, Macey and Buster, jumped onto her bed just at that moment. Macey licked Becky's cheek and Buster nuzzled her shoulder. Becky smiled and began petting her pets. Both dogs wagged their tails, then started jumping around. They were romping and playing all over her bed.

"Calm down, boys. Calm down," said Becky giggling. "You guys always can make me laugh. It feels good to have something to laugh about today. Thank you, Macey. Thank you, Buster. What would I ever do without you guys?"

Reader: Pause. Ask the children the following questions, then continue reading the story.

Can pets help you feel happy when you are sad? (Yes.)

How? (Just like friends, pets can listen to you talk out your problems and comfort you just by being next to you. They can cheer you up by playing with you.)

Then Becky sat up and started talking to her pets. "Hey, do you remember the day we got you two? I sure do. Mom was driving me to school and we saw you both on the side of the road about a mile up from our house. You were just little puppies. Do you remember that day, guys?" Becky asked, as if she expected them to answer.

"I worried about you two all day and I was so happy to see you again when we were driving home from school. I remember Mother slowed the car down so we could look at you both. We were shocked at how skinny and sickly you looked. Mom went straight home and got some thick gloves and a box to put you in. Then we went back to get you. You wagged your tails as Mom carefully picked you up and put you in the box.

"Mom wouldn't let me touch you until we took you to the vet. That's where we went next. The veterinarian gave you some shots and medicine and said that with some tender love and care, plus good food, you would both be as good as new! I was sure glad to hear that.

"The next afternoon, we asked everyone in the neighborhood if anyone had lost their puppies. When no one claimed you, we decided that someone must have made the cruel decision to leave you to take care of yourselves. I can't believe anyone could be so mean! After several trips to the vet and many bowls of water and food, you both were just perfect. You still are," said Becky as she rubbed behind the dogs' ears. "Whoever left you sure made a terrible decision, and I'm glad Mom made the wonderful decision to get you and keep you."

Reader: Pause. Ask the children the following questions, then continue reading the story.

Why did Becky's mother wear thick gloves when she put the dogs into the box to carry them to the vet? (She put on thick gloves in case the puppies tried to bite her. If they did try to bite her, the thick gloves would help protect her.)

Why wouldn't Becky's mother let Becky touch the dogs until the veterinarian had seen them? (People should be careful when handling or petting animals they don't know very well. If you don't know an animal very well, you don't know if it will try to bite you. If the animal did bite you and had not had its shots from the veterinarian, the bite could make you very sick. Becky's mother was just protecting Becky to make sure she would not be bitten.)

With both dogs snuggled up close to her, Becky began to think, "I shouldn't be upset about not being at school with my Valentine friends, because I have two wonderful Valentine friends right here. Macey and Buster are my Valentine friends today!"

Becky continued to think about her pets. "Macey and Buster are doing all the things a Valentine should do. They are making me feel happy, helping me smile and laugh, and showing me they care about me."

Suddenly, Becky felt much happier. "Macey and Buster, you are my Valentine buddies today. Would you want me to be *your* Valentine buddy?"

Then Becky thought some more, "Macey and Buster are always being like Valentine friends to me and I am not always like a Valentine friend to them. So right here and now I am deciding that I am always going to be like a Valentine friend to them. I know Mom and Dad have been the ones to see that Macey and Buster were taken care of, but I am old enough now to do a lot of those things myself."

Becky got up and went into the laundry room. Becky's mother was the one who fed Macey and Buster, but Becky knew this was something she could do on her own for her Valentine friends. She checked Macey and Buster's food and water. She put fresh water in their water bowls and gave them a scoop of dog food.

When Becky looked outside, she thought of other things she could do to help her Valentine friends. She noticed their doghouses under the big tree in the back yard. "I am old enough to change the blankets in their doghouses so they will have fresh, clean bedding. I can help with their baths, too. And … I could help with their daily walks. I could at least walk with Mom or Dad and hold their leashes. I think it is important to take care of pets, so I am making the critical decision right now to be a part of taking care of mine. I want to be a good Valentine to them, like they are to me!"

Reader: Pause. Ask the children the following question, then continue reading the story.

What things did Becky think of that pets need in order to be well taken care of? (Pets need fresh food and water, clean shelter, baths, and exercise.)

As Becky turned and walked back to her bedroom to rest, Macey and Buster followed her every step. Becky stopped to pet them and picked up some of their toys. When she got back into bed, she threw the toys, one by one, and laughed as she watched Macey and Buster scamper wildly to bring them back to her. After several games, Becky calmed her pets down by petting them softly and gently.

"I'm glad I have you to be my Valentines," Becky said as she continued to pet Macey and Buster. "I want you to know that I will always help take care of you and make sure I help you be as happy as you make me."

Reader: Pause. Ask the children the following questions, then continue reading the story.

Do you think Becky is happy that she has made the critical decision to care for her pets? (Yes.)

Why? (She knows that her pets help her, so she should help them.)

Becky's mother looked in and smiled as she heard Becky say cheerfully to her pets, "Happy Valentine's Day, friends!" Mother knew that Becky was able to have a good Valentine's Day after all, thanks to Macey and Buster and thanks to her making the critical decision to care for them.

Name _____

 # MY PET

THIS IS A PICTURE OF MY PET.

My pet's name is _____ .

One thing I do to care for my pet is _____

_____ .

THE CRITICAL DECISION TO GET HELP WHEN YOU ARE BEING BULLIED

Lesson Plan Objectives:

1. Read the story to the children for the purpose of teaching them about the importance of making the critical decision to seek help when they are being bullied.

2. Discuss the questions before or after reading the story to encourage thinking/talking about the results of choosing to get help when being bullied.

3. Select one or more follow-up activities to give children practical experiences in dealing with a bully.

 **LESSON**

Introduction:

▸ Materials needed: Bag of candy for the leader.

▸ Begin the lesson by holding a bag of candy for the children to see. Then ask:

> *What are some ways someone could take this bag of candy from me?* (Someone could sneak up behind you and grab it when you weren't expecting it, someone could tickle you and make you let go of the bag, someone could trick you into dropping the bag by telling you there was a spider on the bag of candy, and any other appropriate answers. A child might say that someone could just politely ask you to share the candy in the bag with him/her.)

> *What would be the nicest way to get the bag of candy?* (The nicest way to get the bag of candy would be to ask politely for you to share the candy.)

▸ Continue the lesson by asking the children to discuss:

Why do people sometimes not think about being kind to others? (Accept any appropriate answers.)

Why do people steal from, act hateful toward, or repeatedly trick other people? (Some reasons the children could give for bullying are: Some people are not taught how to be kind. Sometimes people feel bad about themselves and want to make others feel bad, too. Sometimes people just choose to act in hurtful ways.)

▸ Tell the children:

When people threaten or are very mean to a person, that is called bullying.

Story:

▸ Introduce the story by saying:

Bullies can be dangerous and it is important to get help. Another word for important *is* critical. *Whenever a bullying incident affects you or you witness a bullying act against another person, you must make a decision about what to do. Deciding what to do in these situations is a critical decision.*

Today you are going to hear a story about a little frog that is faced with a bullying problem and makes the critical decision to get help from some trusted adult frogs. If you listen carefully, you can learn what you should decide to do when you are faced with a bullying problem.

▸ Share the candy with the class.

▸ Read *Bubba, The Bullying Bullfrog* (pages 205-209).

Discussion Questions:

▶ Present the following questions to the children. Remind them of the importance of the critical decision to seek help in bullying situations.

1. *What is a bully?* (A *bully* is someone who is abusive to others either physically or emotionally.)

2. *What might cause bullies to act the way they do?* (Bullies may be emotionally troubled, jealous of others, not have been taught how to be kind, enjoy having power over others who seem weaker than they, want attention, and any other appropriate answers the children may contribute.)

3. *What can a person do if he or she is bullied?* (A person could choose to try ignoring the bully, walking away from the bully, avoiding the bully, staying with a group of trusted friends, telling the bully to leave him/her alone, or talking with the bully. Always tell a trusted adult about the bullying situation.)

4. *Any time a person feels bullied, he or she should seek help from a trusted adult. How can this be done?* (A person could tell an adult, have a friend tell for him/her, leave a note for the adult to read, have his/her parents call the school about what is going on, and any other appropriate answers.)

5. *What should you do if you see someone being bullied?* (You should do something to help. If you would be in danger by helping the bullied person yourself, you should find some way to get help from a trusted adult.)

6. *What should you do if you think you overheard someone talking about doing something harmful to another person?* (Even if you are not sure, you should tell a trusted adult. See the answers to Discussion Question #4 on ways you can tell a trusted adult about a bullying situation.)

7. *What should you do if you thought you saw someone bring a weapon of any kind to school?* (Even if you are not sure, you should tell a trusted adult what you think you saw. See the answers to Discussion Question #4 on ways you can tell a trusted adult.)

8. *What if your best friend makes you promise you won't tell that you heard or saw something dangerous?* (Even if you promised you wouldn't tell, you *must* tell. This is a promise you are allowed to break because breaking the promise could prevent others from being hurt. See the answers to Discussion Question #4 on ways you can tell a trusted adult.)

Follow-Up Activities:

ACTIVITY #1

▸ This activity will give the children practice in dealing with a bullying situation.

▸ Materials needed: None

▸ Through role-playing, show how you could respond to the following situations. (Note: Although suggestions for responses to the role-plays are given, children may want to act out other responses.)

Situation 1:

You will need at least three people to role-play the following scene:

You see Person #1, an older child, picking on Person #2, a much younger child.

How should Person #3, the witness to the bullying situation, respond?

Person #3 could quickly think about ways to help the younger child, then pick the solution that he/she feels most comfortable and safest using.

If Person #3 would be in harm's way by helping the child him/herself, then Person #3 should stay away and seek help from a trusted adult.

Even if Person #3 was not in harm's way and chose to help the child him/herself, Person #3 should tell a trusted adult what happened.

Situation 2:

You will need at least two people to role-play the following scene:

Person #1 has been calling Person #2 mean names at recess.

How should Person #2 respond to the bullying situation?

Person #2 could stay with friends who are kind to him/her and stay away from Person #1, who is a bully.

Person #2 could ignore the bully and walk away from Person #1.

Person #2 could get help from a trusted adult.

Situation 3:

You will need at least three people to role-play the following scene:

Person #1 overhears Person #2 and Person #3 talking on the school bus. They are saying they are going to beat up someone when they get to school.

How should Person #1, who is a witness, respond?

Person #1 should get the information to a trusted adult so the fight will be prevented.

Situation 4:

You will need at least three people to role-play the following scene:

Person #1, a bigger kid, cuts in front of Person #2 in line.

How should Person #2 respond to the bullying situation?

Person #2 could choose to tell Person #1 to get back where he/she belongs.

If Person #2 does not feel safe telling this to Person #1, Person #2 should get this information to a trusted adult so the line can be monitored in the future.

Situation 5:

You will need at least two people to role-play the following scene:

Person #1 sees Person #2 put a weapon into his/her backpack and take it to school. Person #2 threatens to beat up Person #1 if he/she tells anyone about the weapon.

How should Person #1 respond to the bullying situation?

As soon as possible, Person #1 should get this information to a trusted adult to prevent someone from being hurt.

ACTIVITY #2

▸ This activity will help the children brainstorm possible options when faced with a bullying situation.

▸ Materials needed: Chalkboard and chalk or dry-eraser board and marker for the leader.

▸ Write the word BULLY vertically on the board. Then, as a class, discuss the options that can be chosen when faced with a bullying situation. Below is a suggested example.

Be firm and tell the bully to stop and leave you alone.

Understand there is usually an underlying problem with the bully.

Look at the options you have in dealing with the bully and choose the option you feel most comfortable and safest using.

Leave the bully and stay with your friends.

You should always seek help from a trusted adult in dealing with a bully.

ACTIVITY #3

▶ This activity will give the children another source to support their critical decision to get help from a trusted adult when faced with a bullying situation. It will also help them learn the consequences of bullying.

▶ Materials needed: None

▶ Invite a prison guard or a police officer to come to your class to explain the consequences of choosing to be a bully.

▶ Explain that bullies who do not learn how to get along with other people will not be able to function well in society and could even end up in jail.

ACTIVITY #4

▶ This activity will celebrate the children's critical decision to not bully and to get help if a bully is mean to them.

▶ Materials needed: None

▶ Teach the children the following song, sung to the tune of *"This Little Light Of Mine."*

> *I won't be a bully, NO!*
> *I am going to be kind.*
> *I won't be a bully, NO!*
> *I am going to be kind.*
> *Going to be kind.*
> *Going to be kind.*
> *Going to be kind.*
>
> *I will follow the Golden Rule.* (Treat others the way you want to be treated.)
> *I am going to be kind.*
> *I will follow the Golden Rule.*
> *I am going to be kind.*
> *Going to be kind.*
> *Going to be kind.*
> *Going to be kind.*

I will be a friend, OH, YES!
I am going to be kind.
I will be a friend, OH, YES!
I am going to be kind.
Going to be kind.
Going to be kind.
Going to be kind.

(CHILD'S NAME) is very kind.
(SHE/HE) is very kind.
(CHILD'S NAME) is very kind.
(SHE/HE) is very kind.
Very kind.
Very kind.
Very kind.

▸ You may wish to have the children sit in a circle and sing the last verse about each child. The child who is being sung about could stand in the middle of the circle. You could divide the class into two circles if you do not want the activity to last too long. This way, two children could be sung about at once.

BUBBA, THE BULLYING BULLFROG

Bubba Bullfrog was a lucky frog. He had a deep, croaky voice. He could be heard singing across the whole pond. He also had strong, muscular legs. He could jump from one lily pad to another lily pad even if the pads were very far apart. Lastly, he was extremely quick at catching flies. Whenever the annual fly-catching contest came around, the other frogs just concentrated on who could get second place. They all knew Bubba Bullfrog would always come in first.

Bubba Bullfrog was proud of himself. The other frogs would have been proud of him, too, but Bubba did not use his talents in a nice way. Let me tell you what he did.

When Bubba Bullfrog woke up, he would start his loud croaking even if the other frogs were still sleeping. He would make his croaks loud and bossy. He would croak in his deep voice, "Wake up, sleepy slimeheads! Get up or I'll kick you with my strong legs." He wasn't fooling! Sometimes he would leap over to where they were snoozing—or at least trying to snooze—and kick them to get them up. And it wouldn't stop there. All the frogs would be hungry for breakfast and Bubba, because he was much faster than they, would race ahead and catch most of the best flies. Then he would laugh and say they were slow pokey sleepyheads.

He sometimes would even kick some of the smaller frogs out of the way to get the flies that were close to their lily pads. The other frogs started calling him Bully Bubba Bullfrog because he was so much of a bully to everyone.

They did not know what to do. They had tried ignoring Bubba Bullfrog, but this did not help at all. They had tried being firm and telling him, "Leave us alone!" That did not work, either. Nothing they had thought to try seemed to help their situation.

Reader: Pause. Ask the children the following question, then continue reading the story.

So far in our story, how has Bubba Bullfrog acted like a bully? (He has called other frogs names, stolen their flies, kicked them, and wakened them when they were sleeping.)

One day, Merry Mary Bullfrog spoke up and said, "Something needs to be done! This can't go on! We are all afraid and miserable because of Bully Bubba Bullfrog. What are we going to do about this?"

Everyone agreed it was a miserable situation and started talking about their horrible predicament.

Then they started brainstorming about what else they could try. They discussed fighting back, but decided this was too dangerous. They discussed leaving their pond, but they knew there was not another pond for miles and miles.

Then Merry Mary Bullfrog spoke up again. She said, "I think we need to decide to get help. It is high time we tell some trusted adult frogs in our pond what has been going on. There is no reason to keep this a secret any more, because we definitely need some help!"

Reader: Pause. Ask the children the following questions, then continue reading the story.

Do you think it is a critical decision for the little frogs to tell an adult frog? (Yes.)

Why? (They need help from an adult because Bubba is bullying them and because they stand a chance of getting hurt.)

Everyone agreed with Mary. That very evening, all of the little frogs went to an adult they could trust to help them and told the whole story. They told what they had been trying to do to stop Bubba Bullfrog and said that nothing seemed to be working.

The adult listened to what the little frogs said. She did not blame them for anything and did not look at them like they were weak or like they were making a big deal out of nothing. She believed them and wanted to help.

The very next day, she called all the adult frogs in the pond to meet and discuss what could be done. At their meeting, they worked on a plan to stop Bubba Bullfrog from bullying any more.

"First," spoke one of the adult frogs, "we need to have someone talk with Bubba and try to find out why he is being a bully."

"Secondly," stated another adult frog, "we need to explain to Bubba that his threatening actions will not be tolerated."

"I agree," another adult frog said. "And thirdly, we need to think of some consequences for Bubba if he does not stop bullying."

"Good idea," remarked another adult frog. "We could have him clean and polish our lily pads every time he does a bullying action."

The adult bullfrogs all liked the ideas they were coming up with. They were making a good plan.

"One more thing," stated still another adult frog. "We need to station ourselves in the areas of the pond where Bubba seems to do most of his bullying. That way, we will have a chance to prevent some of his bullying."

We little frogs are so glad that we told," said Merry Mary Bullfrog. "We could tell the adult frogs really cared about us and wanted to help us. We knew we had done the right thing by telling them and not keeping it a secret any more."

The adult bullfrogs started carrying out their plan. It immediately seemed to make some difference right away.

Uncle Jim Bullfrog volunteered to talk with Bubba. Uncle Jim was very good at helping frogs, so his talks with Bubba went well. Uncle Jim found out that Bubba really had a lot of problems of his own.

Uncle Jim told Bubba, "I promise I will help you work through your problems. You can come and talk with me any time."

Then Uncle Jim Bullfrog explained what would happen if Bubba continued to bully others.

When Bubba seemed to understand, the little frogs became very confident that everything would finally work out.

And it did. After the little frogs told the adults, and after the adults made a plan to help them, Bubba Bullfrog didn't have to be called a *bully* any more.

Uncle Jim helped Bubba stop bullying and get involved in something nice. Bubba now sings in the frog choir and teaches karate to some of the little frogs. He even helped one of the little frogs with his fly-catching skills one evening. With help from everyone, Bubba had made a change for the better.

Bubba Bullfrog learned a lesson and so did the little frogs. Bubba learned that bullying would get him into trouble. The little frogs learned that they should always make the critical decision to tell an adult if someone is bullying them. Thanks to their telling and the adults' help, life in their pond couldn't be any better.

The little frogs made a critical decision when they decided to tell and get some help.

THE CRITICAL DECISION TO
SET GOALS

Lesson Plan Objectives:

1. Read the story to the children for the purpose of teaching them about the importance of making the critical decision to set goals.

2. Discuss the questions before or after reading the story to encourage thinking/talking about the results of choosing to set goals.

3. Select one or more follow-up activities to give children practical experiences in setting goals.

 **LESSON**

Introduction:

▸ Materials needed: Piece of art paper, piece of lined paper, a pencil, and crayons for each child.

▸ Distribute the art paper, a pencil, and crayons to each child. Ask the children to draw a picture of themselves doing the job they want to be doing when they are an adult. When everyone has finished, have the children share their pictures with the class.

▸ Then say:

> *Wanting a grown-up job is a long-term goal, because it will take a long time to finally reach that goal. However, there are short-term goals that you can be working on right now to help you get this job.*

▸ Continue the lesson by asking:

> *Do you think doing well in school would help you get the job you want? (Yes.)*

Why? (Because a future employer would want someone who knows at least the basics of reading, writing, and math.)

What do you think would help you do well in school so you can get the job you want later in life? (Studying, doing homework, getting along well with others, being respectful to the teachers, and any other appropriate answer.)

▶ Then say: (Note: Some children may have to be reminded that all jobs: race car drivers, basketball players, baseball players, construction workers, etc. require basic academic skills in reading, writing, and math.)

If you keep in mind what you want to accomplish and work toward reaching your goals, you will have a better chance of succeeding and making your dreams come true.

Race car drivers must read the instructions of racing, write out plans on how to win races, and do math when it comes to the money they make and the bills that must be paid.

Basketball players have to read ball drills for winning a game, write out plans for winning a game, do math when it comes to the money they make and bills that must be paid.

Story:

▶ Introduce the story by saying:

Setting goals is important. It is a decision that each person must make about his or her own life. Since another word for important *is* critical, *making goals is a critical decision.*

Today you are going to hear a story about a character that makes the critical decision to set goals in order to accomplish things in his life. If you listen closely, you will better understand the importance of deciding to set goals for your life.

▶ Read *Hippity Hop Rabbit Learns About Goals* (pages 216-222).

Discussion Questions:

▸ Present the following questions to the children. Remind them of the importance of the critical decision to set goals.

1. *Why do you think people make goals or resolutions for themselves on New Year's day?* (Since the new year represents a new beginning, people think of this time as a chance to make a fresh start and do better with their lives.)

2. *Can people make goals or resolutions any time of the year?* (Yes.)

3. *How do goals help people do better?* (Goals motivate people to accomplish things because they help people focus and be determined about things they want to accomplish.)

4. *What are short-term goals?* (Short-term goals are goals that take a short amount of time to accomplish. Examples of short-term goals are: getting a cake baked for your brother's birthday, making a good grade on your spelling test this Friday, or winning the ballgame this weekend.)

5. *What are long-term goals?* (Long-term goals are goals that take a long amount of time to accomplish. Examples of long-term goals are: becoming an astronaut when you are grown, being undefeated in all baseball games this season, or making a quilt with your grandmother.)

6. *What could happen if a person does not set goals?* (A person who does not set specific goals for him/herself is likely to not accomplish very many things in his/her life.)

7. *How does a person go about setting a goal?* (Accept any appropriate answers, then review the steps for setting goals.)

▸ Distribute a piece of lined paper to each child. Review the following steps for setting goals by saying:

Think of a few (3-5) important things that you would like to do or accomplish. These could be either long- or short-term goals.

Write these goals down on paper in the following way:

- *Write down your goals as if you are already working toward them.*

- *Write down specific steps to take to reach each goal.*

For example: Instead of saying, "I want to do better in math," say, "I will do better in math because I will study at least 10-15 minutes each evening." If you write a goal in this manner, reading it over and over will encourage you to continue to work to accomplish your goal.

Read your goals out loud to yourself each day. This will help you stay focused on what you want to accomplish and what you must do to accomplish them.

Examples of short-term goals include:

- *I have a neat bedroom because I clean my room each Friday afternoon after school.*

- *I finished my book report book because I read at least a chapter each night before I went to bed.*

Examples of long-term goals include:

- *I finished the quilt that my grandmother was helping me with by visiting her and working with her each Sunday evening for at least an hour.*

- *I am a star basketball player because I never miss a practice and because I practice basketball each evening for at least an hour.*

Follow-Up Activities:

ACTIVITY #1

▸ This activity will give the children practice in wording their goals in a positive and encouraging fashion.

▸ Materials needed: None

▸ Have the children change each of the following goal statements so it is written as if the person is already working toward the goal. Include the specific steps that must be taken to reach the goal.

- I hope I will save enough money to buy a new video game.

    I have saved enough money to buy the video game because I asked my parents if I could do extra jobs around the house. I put the money I earned in the bank until I had saved enough to buy the video game I wanted.

- I hope I will do well on my math test.

    I did well on my math test because I asked my teacher to help me with the things I did not understand and I studied for at least 20 minutes each evening after supper.

- I wish my sister and I would get along better.

    My sister and I get along better now because I compliment her every day and do not argue with her.

ACTIVITY #2

▸ This activity will help children feel proud of themselves.

▸ Materials needed: None

▸ Ask the children to describe two or three goals that they have already accomplished. Some sample answers could be:

- For older children: (I have learned to skate, learned to ride a bike, learned to ski, learned to add and subtract, learned to write a sentence, learned to count in Spanish, learned to play dominoes, made a model car.)

- For younger children: (I have learned the ABCs, learned to write my name, learned numbers, learned to read, learned my part in a puppet play, made a Valentine Box, made a good grade on a spelling test, stayed the night with someone without being homesick.)

▶ After the children have described their accomplishments, encourage them by saying:

If you have already accomplished so much, just imagine how much more you are capable of accomplishing if you set your mind to doing other things! I am proud of you and amazed at all you have done in your lives so far.

ACTIVITY #3

▶ This activity will give the children plans to start and keep working on their goals.

▶ Materials needed: Paper and a pencil or crayons for each child.

▶ Distribute paper and a pencil or crayons to each child. Have the children write down two or three goals they want to accomplish. Instruct them to write their goals as explained in the goal-setting review.

Younger children who cannot write well may draw two or three pictures on paper. Allow time for the children to share their pictures and guide the younger children to describe their goals as modeled in the goal-setting review.

HIPPITY HOP RABBIT LEARNS ABOUT GOALS

Ring, ring, ring went Jumpity Jump's phone.

"Hello," said Jumpity Jump Rabbit.

"Hope you had a happy New Year," Hippity Hop Rabbit said to his friend. "I was calling to see if you wanted to come over and watch TV with me today."

"I would love to later, if that is OK. I'm busy right now going over the goals I made for myself for this new year," answered Jumpity Jump.

"Goals?" questioned Hippity Hop Rabbit.

"Yes, goals," replied Jumpity. "I make resolutions or goals each new year so I can make sure I am accomplishing what I want to in my life. What are you doing?"

"Me? Oh, nothing is up with me. I'm lying on my couch. I plan to just relax and watch TV," said Hippity Hop. "I don't like to make plans or set goals for myself. I like to enjoy myself as much as possible and just let the days come and go as they may."

"I like to enjoy myself, too," responded Jumpity Jump. "But you know what? I've found that accomplishing goals is a very enjoyable thing to do. Each goal that I finally reach makes me feel proud of myself and that makes me happy."

"To each his own," replied Hippity Hop. "It doesn't sound like fun to me. But after you finish what you are doing, why don't you stop by and watch a TV program or two?"

"That sounds good to me. I'll see you later," said Jumpity Jump.

After hanging up the phone, Jumpity Jump continued going over the goals he had set for himself for the new year.

"OK," he said to himself, "one of my short-term goals can be accomplished today. The goal I wrote states: My screen door works properly because I tightened the screws on the hinges to keep the door from dragging."

After reading this goal, Jumpity Jump got his screwdriver and began tightening the screws on the hinges. Then he was ready to test his work. Jumpity opened and closed the screen door and saw that it did not drag any more.

"Yeah," Jumpity congratulated himself. "I am glad I got that done. The dragging of the door was beginning to get on my nerves.

"What is next on my list of things to do?" Jumpity asked looking at what he had written. "Oh, I see another short-term goal that I could accomplish. The goal I wrote states: My bike works well because I oiled the chain.

"OK, here's the oil," said Jumpity. "I will just squeeze a bit onto the chain." When he had finished, Jumpity gave his pedals a turn. "Yes, much, much better. This will keep my chain from rusting and will make my bike ride great."

Jumpity was proud of himself and looked at what else was on his list to do. "OK, I see a long-term goal that I need to get started on. The goal reads: I am in good shape because I exercise at least three times a week for twenty minutes."

"OK, I need to exercise," said Jumpity. "That's easy. I know what I will do. I will jog over to see my friend Hippity Hop."

Reader: Pause. Ask the children the following questions, then continue reading the story.

Do you think Jumpity Jump is accomplishing a lot? (Yes.)

What has helped him accomplish so much? (He is accomplishing a lot because he has made the critical decision to set goals and to work on reaching them.)

Jumpity jogged over to Hippity Hop Rabbit's house and knocked on the door, "Knock, knock! Hippity Hop, are you home?"

CRITICAL DECISIONS © 2006 MAR+CO PRODUCTS, INC. 1-800-448-2197

Hippity Hop Rabbit went to the door. He tried to open his door to let his friend in, but the door would not budge.

"The door will not open, Jumpity," said Hippity Hop Rabbit trying to push it open. "I'm stuck in here."

"Stuck?" questioned Jumpity Jump. "What is going on?"

"I kept meaning to fix my door lock. The lock has been sticking, but now it is STUCK! I can't get out," Hippity Hop Rabbit yelled through the door to his friend. "Can you help me?"

"Don't panic Hippity," answered Jumpity. "I'll help you, but I wish you had fixed the door lock before it got so bad."

"I do, too," answered Hippity Hop Rabbit, "but I didn't and now I need you to help me. Get me out!"

Jumpity Jump found a wedge tool in Hippity Hop Rabbit's garage and proceeded to pry open the door. Finally, the door opened and Hippity was freed.

"Yeah! Thank you! Thank you! Thank you! I am so glad I am not trapped any more," exclaimed Hippity Hop Rabbit.

"No problem," said Jumpity Jump. "But I did mess up your door with the wedge. Your lock is completely broken now. I'll take the door down and we can pull it to the store in your wagon. You will also need to have a new lock put on after your door is repaired.

"Uuuuhhh, good idea, except we can't use my wagon. One of the wheels fell off a few weeks ago," said Hippity Hop Rabbit.

"Why haven't you put it back on?" questioned Jumpity Jump.

"I keep meaning to, but I keep forgetting to do it," answered Hippity Hop Rabbit.

"OK," replied Jumpity Jump. "We can run back to my house and use my wagon to pull the door to the store."

"If you don't mind, Jumpity Jump, I'll just wait here while you get your wagon," said Hippity Hop Rabbit. "My favorite TV show is about to come on. I'm kind of tired, too."

"Tired? You haven't done anything to make you tired," exclaimed Jumpity Jump. "And as far as watching TV, you have things you need to be doing. You don't have time to sit and watch TV today."

Jumpity Jump tried to be patient and explain what Hippity Hop Rabbit needed to do.

Reader: Pause. Ask the children the following question, then continue reading the story.

What do you think Hippity Hop Rabbit needs to do? (He needs to make the critical decision to set goals and work to make things better.)

"Listen to me, Hippity. I think it is time you learned to make a list of goals. You and your property are falling apart. If you don't get it together, you are going to be in a worse mess in the near future," said Jumpity Jump.

"Yeah," Hippity Hop Rabbit agreed. "I know. I guess you are right. Things around here are starting to be a mess. I need to learn how to get organized and start getting some things done. Can you help me?"

"I sure can! I am glad you want to get some help. And since it is just the start of the new year, this is a perfect time to make goals to get yourself and your things into shape. Come on, now. Let's go inside and start working on some short-term and long-term goals," said Jumpity Jump.

CRITICAL DECISIONS © 2006 MAR★CO PRODUCTS, INC. 1-800-448-2197

After he explained that a short-term goal was one he could accomplish in the near future, Jumpity Jump asked Hippity Hop Rabbit what short-term goals he wanted to make. Hippity Hop Rabbit said he wanted his wagon and his door and lock fixed.

Jumpity Jump wrote down Hippity Hop Rabbits's goals. He wrote:

1. My wagon works properly because I put the wheel back on after it had fallen off.

2. My door and lock work properly because I took the door to be repaired and bought a new lock.

Then Jumpity Jump explained that long-term goals are goals that may take a long time to reach. Hippity Hop Rabbit said he would like to take a gardening class offered this year and do well in it, and would like to have more energy. Jumpity Jump talked with Hippity Hop Rabbit about these goals, then wrote this for his friend:

1. I am enrolled in my gardening class and doing well because I go to class every day and study each evening for at least one hour.

2. I have energy because I am in good shape. I exercise with Jumpity Jump at least three times a week.

When the goals were written down, Hippity Hop Rabbit said, "Thank you Jumpity Jump for helping me learn how to write down my goals for now and for my future."

Reader: Pause. Ask the children the following questions, then continue reading the story.

Do you think Hippity Hop Rabbit has learned the importance of goal-setting? (Yes.)

How can you tell? (He listened to Jumpity Jump and set his goals. He also thanked his friend for telling him about goals.)

"You are welcome, Hippity. I am proud of you. I think you are going to have a bright new year," Jumpity Jump said. "It was fun helping you. I enjoyed it."

"I am excited about getting all these things accomplished. You were right, Jumpity Jump. Goals *can* be fun." said Hippity Hop Rabbit. "Let's get started right away."

"Sure thing," said Jumpity Jump. "We'll get started right now. We can start by taking that jog to get my wagon in order for you to have a door and a lock that works properly."

"I'm ready," replied Hippity Hop Rabbit, as he began to hop along the path to Jumpity Jump's house.

Both friends smiled. They were both proud of their critical decision to set goals for themselves. Both friends knew this was a start of a wonderful new year!

THE CRITICAL DECISION TO
BE CAREFUL OF STRANGER DANGERS

Lesson Plan Objectives:

1. Read the story to the children for the purpose of teaching them about the importance of making the critical decision to be careful of stranger dangers.

2. Discuss the questions before or after reading the story to encourage thinking/talking about the results of choosing to be careful of stranger dangers.

3. Select one or more follow-up activities to give children practical experiences in being aware of stranger dangers.

⊚⊚⊚⊚ LESSON ⊚⊚⊚⊚

Introduction:

▸   Materials needed: Magazine pictures of pretty/handsome people and pictures of people who look scary or hateful for the leader.

▸   Show the pictures, one at a time, to the class. When you hold up each picture, ask the children to signal *thumbs-up* if they think the person in the picture is a stranger and to signal *thumbs-down* if they do not think the person in the picture is a stranger. (Note: Children will often say only the scary or hateful-looking people in the pictures are strangers and that the pretty/handsome people in the pictures are *not* strangers.)

▸   After displaying all the pictures and getting the children's opinions on whether the people in the pictures are strangers, say:

> *ALL the people in the pictures are STRANGERS because you do NOT know them.*

It is important to remember that a mean stranger could be very pretty or handsome and, as a matter of fact, probably would be because he or she would want to trick children into thinking he or she was nice by looking sweet and handsome or pretty.

A stranger *is anyone you and your family don't know REALLY well. A stranger can be a boy or girl, pretty or handsome, young or old, clean or dirty.*

Almost everyone who is a stranger is a good person, but there are a few people who are not good. That is why the ONLY way you know if someone is safe to be with is if you and your family really know the person VERY well.

If you are faced with a stranger situation, you must decide what to do. This is an important decision. Another word for important *is* critical. Deciding to follow Stranger Danger Safety Rules is a critical decision.

Story:

▶ Introduce the story by saying:

> Today you are going to hear a story about a little boy who is going to make the critical decision to follow Stranger Danger Safety Rules. If you listen carefully, you will learn that making the critical decision to follow the Stranger Danger Safety Rules will help keep you safe.

▶ Read *George Learns The Stranger Danger Safety Rules* (pages 230-236).

Discussion Questions:

▶ Present the following questions to the children. Remind them of the importance of the critical decision to be careful of stranger dangers.

1. *Who is a* stranger? (A *stranger* is someone you and your family do not know very well.)

2. *Should you talk with, take gifts from, help, or go anywhere with a stranger?* (No.)

    Why? (You should not talk with, take gifts from, help, or go anywhere with a stranger because the stranger could be mean and could hurt you in some way.)

3. *What are some tricks that mean strangers might use to try to get you to go with them?* (A mean stranger might ask, "Will you help me find my lost dog, please?; offer you candy to go with him/her to his/her car; ask you to help get something from his/her van; try to trick you by saying you won a prize and if you go with him/her, you will get the prize; say that your parent/guardian is sick and that you are to go with him/her and see your sick parent/guardian.)

    (Note: Leaders may want to explain that parents/guardians would never send a stranger to pick up a child and that children should never go anywhere with a stranger, no matter what he/she says.)

4. *What should you do if a stranger grabs you and says he or she is going to hurt you if you try to get away?* (You should try to get away anyway. You should kick, bite, yell, hit, and shout, "I don't know this person! HELP!" Remember: You would be in worse danger if you stayed with the stranger. You would need to do whatever you could to get away from the stranger.)

5. *What should you do after you get away from a stranger who was trying to get you to go with him or her?* (You should run to a trusted adult to tell him/her what has happened. You could also call 911 and tell the operator what has happened to you.)

6. *What can you do to protect yourself from mean strangers?* (Accept any appropriate answers.)

If not suggested by the children, discuss the following examples of ways to protect oneself from strangers. Say:

> *If you are lost and alone in a mall or store, ask someone that is working behind a counter to help you. Do not ask a stranger to help you.*

If you are home alone, lock all doors and windows. Do not answer the door for anyone unless you know the person very well. A mean stranger could dress like a police officer or repairperson to trick you into letting him or her into your house.

If you are home alone and the phone rings, tell the caller that your parent(s) cannot come to the phone. Do not tell the caller that you are alone. Tell the person on the phone that you can take a message.

If you are being followed by a stranger or a stranger tries to talk to you, keep your distance so the stranger cannot grab you. Do not talk to the stranger. Run to a neighbor's house or a place of business for help.

If you are home alone and need help about what to do about a stranger, call 911 and tell the operator your problem. Be ready to tell the operator your name and address.

A stranger may try many tricky things to get you to go with him or her. Do not be tricked. Never leave with a stranger. Some tricks a stranger could try are:

- asking for your address so he or she can mail you a prize
- asking for your help in finding a lost puppy
- saying your parents have been in an accident and he or she will take you to the hospital to see them.

Do not wear or carry things with your name on them. This will tell strangers your name and they can pretend to know you.

Try to always walk in well-lighted and well-traveled areas. Try to always walk with one or more other people.

Tell a trusted adult where you are going and when you will be back.

If a stranger grabs you, kick, bite, scratch, and yell, "Help, I don't know this person!" Get away from the stranger no matter what he or she tells you or does.

CRITICAL DECISIONS © 2006 MAR*CO PRODUCTS, INC. 1-800-448-2197

Remember: A stranger will probably try to appear sweet and nice. Don't fall for a stranger's tricks.

7.   *There are some areas on your body that should only be touched by a doctor or a parent or guardian when washing or helping you when you are hurt or sick. What are these areas on your body? (The areas on your body that are private parts are the areas that you cover up with a bathing suit. If anyone touches you in these areas and makes you feel uncomfortable, tell a trusted adult.)*

Follow-Up Activities:

ACTIVITY #1

▸   This activity will be fun and encourage children to remember the lesson about stranger dangers.

▸   Materials needed: Homemade sack puppet for each child.

▸   Put on a puppet play. Instead of store-bought puppets, you could have a "sack-puppet" play. Ask the children to decorate a sack puppet with the help of a parent/guardian. If you decide to do this, send a note home asking parents/guardians to help children decorate a sack to look like a boy or girl of any age. Explain that the sack puppets will be used in a puppet play.

(Note: The children will enjoy doing this at home and the activity will, hopefully, stir up interest in the play from the children and their parents/guardians.)

▸   If some parents/guardians are unable to help with this project, plan to set aside some time for those who need a sack and some assistance from you.

▸   The puppet play is divided into seven sections. Divide the children into groups of three or four and have each group do its part behind a long table or curtain. Assign each child a line or two to say with his/her puppet.

Play Section #1
1. Most people are nice, kind, and true.
2. Most people care about me … and you.
3. But there are a few people out there who are mean and don't care!
4. So stay away from strangers. Beware! Beware!

Play Section #2
5. You don't know which stranger
6. Is good or bad.
7. So stay away from strangers!
8. Stick with your mom or dad!

Play Section #3
9. If a stranger comes to you looking nice or looking mean,
10. If a stranger offers you candy or even ice cream,
11. If a stranger asks you to come with her and go, go, go,
12. The answer to all of these is NO, NO, NO!

Play Section #4
13. If approached by a stranger, don't talk or stick around.
14. Run, run, run away and scream very loud!
15. Yell, "Help" or "I don't know this guy!"
16. Run, scream, and yell—and it's OK to cry.

Play Section #5
17. Remember to never leave with strangers.
18. Never let their tricks—trick you!
19. Get away from strangers,
20. No matter what they do!

Play Section #6
21. Stranger Danger!
22. We've learned a lot!
23. We know whom we can trust
24. And whom we cannot!

Play Section #7
25. You're smart about strangers now
26. And we're all proud of you!
27. So let's just pass this word on through ...
28. Tell your friends and your kinfolks, too.
29. Stay away from strangers
30. It's the smart thing to do!

Thank you for coming to our play. We hope you learned a lot and enjoyed seeing us perform.

ACTIVITY #2

▶ This activity will give the children practice in remembering what to do if approached by a stranger.

▶ Materials needed: None

▶ Have groups of children role-play:

- What they would do if a stranger tried to get them to talk or leave with him/her.

- What a stranger might do to trick someone into talking and leaving with him/her. (Note: See Discussion Questions 3, 4, 5, and 6 for role-play ideas.)

ACTIVITY #3

▶ This activity will give the children another source that will support the critical decision to be careful of stranger dangers.

▶ Materials needed: None

▶ Invite a police officer to talk with the class about stranger dangers.

GEORGE LEARNS THE STRANGER DANGER SAFETY RULES

"Richard, if you are planning to take George trick-or-treating, you probably need to get started soon. I don't want you to miss the school Halloween party later tonight. Both of you be sure and follow all the Stranger Danger Safety Rules," said Richard and George's mother.

"I will, Mom, don't worry. I think I'm old enough to take care of myself and George," replied Richard.

George was excited that his big brother, Richard, had come home from his first year of college to take him trick-or-treating. He could hardly wait to get started.

"Come on, Richard! Let's go!" George said anxiously from under his pirate hat.

"OK, OK, I'm ready," Richard said as he picked George up and sat him on his shoulders. "Button up your pirate jacket on our way out, George. I think it's so cold your pirate eye patch just might freeze to your eyebrow."

As Richard and George ducked to pass under the doorframe, Richard called out, "We'll be back soon, Mom. George is going to get me lots of candy to eat tonight. Right, George?"

"I'm going to get candy for ME to eat tonight," replied George.

"Oh, is *that* how it works? Doggone it!" teased Richard.

George wiggled with excitement. Then he tugged on Richard's ears, saying, "Come on, big brother. Let's go!"

Richard and their mother smiled as the brothers made their way down the driveway to the sidewalk.

"I heard you tell Mom that we are going to follow Stranger Danger Safety Rules tonight. I know what a Stranger Danger Safety Rule is, Richard," said George.

"You do?" Richard was impressed. "What is it?"

"Well, when you get candy from someone, you put it in your trick-or-treat bag and hold onto the bag tightly so no stranger can get your candy!" George said confidently.

Richard smiled and lowered George from his shoulders. "Wow! You sure are smart for a four-year-old. I'll bet you are smart enough to learn more safety rules. What do you think?" asked Richard.

"First, I'm four and one-half. And second, I can learn *anything*!" said George.

"Great," said Richard smiling proudly at George. Richard thought a bit then asked, "What if I teach you eight more rules? That way, you will know two rules for every birthday you have had. OK?"

"OK!" answered George.

"Here we are at Mr. Glendirk's house. Rule 1 to remember is that Mr. Glendirk is someone we know very well, so he is not a stranger. It is safe to ask him for candy," said Richard. "Go up to the door and do your trick-or-treating. I'll watch and wait for you right here on the sidewalk. OK?"

"OK," said George as he went up to Mr. Glendirk's door and took a big handful of candy.

"Great job! You are a great trick-or-treater!" said Richard.

"I know," said George. "I'm ready to do it again! Let's go to that house over there with all the lights and pumpkins in the yard."

"Oh, I'm glad you said this, George. This leads to Rule 2. I think the people who live in that house are probably really nice people. But I don't know this for sure, because I don't know those people very well.

Since I don't know them very well, those people are strangers to us," explained Richard.

"Rule 2 is that we can't take treats of any kind from anyone who is a stranger. If we don't know them very well, we don't know if they are nice or mean. I wouldn't want you to take any candy, or anything else, from a stranger, because a stranger might try to hurt you," continued Richard.

"Why would a stranger try to hurt me?" George asked as he grabbed Richard's hand.

Richard held George's hand and explained, "Most people are nice, but some people choose to be mean. I don't know why some people choose to be mean, but I do know Rule 3 will keep you safe from mean strangers.

"You are safe from strangers because you are walking with me," said Richard. "Rule 3 is that you don't walk alone anywhere and you make sure that where you walk is well-lighted and there are people around. We are following Rule 3, so we are safe. You don't have to worry about anyone hurting you if you follow the Stranger Danger Safety Rules."

"What about Rule 4?" asked George.

"Rule 4," continued Richard, "is that if you are ever alone at home, don't open the door for anyone and don't tell anyone who calls that you are alone. Tell anyone who calls that Mom can't come to the phone, ask who they are, and ask for a number so she can call them back."

George held up one finger and said, "Rule 1 is that we can get candy from Mr. Glendirk because we know him really well and know he is nice." Then George held up two fingers and said, "Rule 2 is we can't get candy, or anything else, from people we don't know really well because they could be mean to us. And Rule 3 is that we always walk in a well-lighted area and we never walk alone. Rule 4 is that I should be very careful if I am home alone."

Do you think George thinks the Stranger Danger Safety Rules Richard is telling him are critical to learn? (Yes.)

How can you tell? (Because George really listened to his brother and concentrated on remembering the rules.)

"George, you amaze me!" said Richard.

Just then, Mrs. Steven drove by with her three children: Billy, Christa, and Angie. Mrs. Steven stopped her car beside Richard and George and asked, "Do you want a ride to school for the Halloween party?"

"Thanks, but we'll walk. We have a few more houses to trick-or-treat before we go to the party," Richard answered.

"OK," replied Mrs. Steven. "We'll see you there later."

Richard and George waved good-bye to Mrs. Steven as she drove off.

"George," said Richard, "this leads to Rule 5. Mrs. Steven is someone we know very well so, when she asked us to leave with her, we could have said yes and been OK. But never leave with a stranger because a stranger could take you away and try to hurt you."

Richard noticed that his younger brother was really listening to what he had to say, so he continued, "This leads to Rule 6. If a stranger grabs you and tries to take you away, you should kick, scream, bite, or do whatever you can to get away. I think you would do well at this, don't you, George? You sure do all these things when we 'play wrestle,' don't you buddy?"

"I sure do!" said George. "I think I could do well at Rule 6."

Richard smiled at George as they went to more houses to trick-or-treat.

"Here is a row of houses where we know a lot of people," said Richard. "You can go to Mr. and Mrs. Adams' house and then to Leah and Betsy's house and then on down to Aunt Vicki and Uncle Seth's house. These are all people we know. I'll watch you and meet you on the sidewalk by each house. Now go and see how much candy you can get!"

George raced ahead and Richard watched carefully as his little brother filled his pumpkin bucket with more and more candy.

After George finished at these houses, he and Richard began walking to the school for the Halloween party. As they walked toward the school, Richard said, "Rule 7 is that if a stranger ever tried to talk to you, give you something, or get you to leave with him or her, you should run quickly and tell a trusted adult or call 911 and tell the operator what had just happened to you."

George listened carefully. Richard was proud of his little brother. He knew that George had learned the basic rules about Stranger Danger.

Reader: Pause. Ask the children the following question, then continue reading the story.

Why do you think Richard is proud of George for learning the Stranger Danger Safety Rules? (He is proud because he knows that learning and making the critical decision to follow these rules will help keep George safe.)

As Richard and George neared the school for the Halloween party, George asked, "Richard, what is Rule 8? You said you would teach me two rules for every birthday. We need one more because I am four and one-half."

Richard smiled at George as they walked up the school sidewalk. "Well," said Richard, "Rule 8 is very important to learn. So listen closely."

George stopped and looked up at Richard. "What is it?"

"Rule 8," said Richard, "is to always remember that your big brother is not a stranger, so you should always share your candy with him." With that, Richard jokingly grabbed George's pumpkin bucket.

"Hey," George laughed, "I don't like that rule." George chased Richard up the steps to the door of the gym where the Halloween party was taking place.

Richard smiled at George, gave him back his bucket, and again lifted George onto his shoulders.

"OK, my smart little pirate brother," said Richard. "I'm glad we know and have made the critical decision to follow the Stranger Danger Safety Rules."

"Me, too," said George as he smiled at his big brother. Then they both went into the gym to have some more safe Halloween fun.

CRITICAL DECISIONS © 2006 MAR*CO PRODUCTS, INC. 1-800-448-2197

THE CRITICAL DECISION TO
SPEND TIME WITH ELDERLY PEOPLE
(Service Learning)

Lesson Plan Objectives:

1. Read the story to the children for the purpose of teaching them about the importance of making the critical decision to do some type of service learning. In this case, service learning involves spending time with elderly people.

2. Discuss the questions before or after reading the story to encourage thinking/talking about the results of choosing to spend time with elderly people.

3. Select one or more follow-up activities to give children practical experiences in spending time with elderly people.

◎◎◎◎ LESSON ◎◎◎◎

Introduction:

▶ Materials needed: Picture of the leader when he/she was very young and a recent photo.

▶ Show the children a picture of yourself when you were very young. Then show a more recent picture of yourself. Ask:

What differences do you see in these two pictures? (They may notice that you were shorter or smaller in the first picture, your hair style was different in the two pictures, and any other appropriate answers.)

What do you see that is the same about the pictures? (It is the same person in both pictures. In both pictures, you have the same color eyes, hair, and skin, and any other appropriate answers.)

▶ Compliment the children on the great job they did in describing the things that were the same and different about you in the two pictures.

▶ Ask the children the following questions. Guide them, if necessary, to answer each question with "*yes.*"

- *Do you think I ever got lonely when I was younger?*
- *Do you think I ever get lonely now that I am older?*
- *Do you think I ever cried when I was younger?*
- *Do you think I ever cry now that I am older?*
- *Do you think I liked to have fun when I was younger?*
- *Do you think I like to have fun now that I am older?*
- *Do you think I ever acted silly when I was younger?*
- *Do you think I ever act silly now that I am older?*
- *Do you think I have a lot of the same feelings now that I had when I was younger?*
- *Do you think I need a lot of the same things now that I needed when I was younger?*
- *Would you say that there are many ways that younger and older people are the same?*

Story:

▶ Introduce the story by saying:

Making the decision to be kind and help others is important. It shows that you are a caring person. Being kind and helping others does not mean only helping and being kind to people your own age. It means being kind and helping persons of any age. Another word for important *is* critical. *Knowing this, we know that making the decision to help people of any age is a critical decision.*

Today you are going to hear a story about a little boy who makes the critical decision to spend time with an elderly person—his grandfather. If you listen carefully, you will learn the importance of making this critical decision.

▶ Read *Captain Calvin's Magic Snow Dance* (pages 242-247).

Discussion Questions:

▸ Present the following questions to the children. Remind them of the importance of the critical decision to spend time with elderly people.

1. *How are older people the same as younger people?* (They both feel sad, happy, mad, silly, etc.; they both need love, friends, food, and shelter; they both like to have fun; and any other appropriate answers.)

2. *Can you be friends with someone who is elderly?* (Yes.)

   What are some things you and an elderly person can do together? (You can do many of the same things that you would do with a young friend, such as talk on the phone; play games; go places like the park, library, or movies; tell jokes and laugh; and read books.)

3. *Older people have lived more years than younger people. Since they have lived longer, they may be able to teach us some things they have learned throughout their years. What are some things that older people can teach younger people?* (They can teach us how things were when they were little, games they played when they were little or songs they learned, wise things they have learned that will help us like advice on how to study and why an education is important, help us with problems we are having because they may have overcome some of the same problems, tell us about historical events that happened when they were younger, etc.)

4. *Sometimes older people need help doing things. Should we help them?* (Yes.)

   What are some things we could help older people with? (If they have trouble seeing, we can read things for them; if they have trouble walking, we can help them get around; if they have trouble carrying things, we can carry something for them; if they have trouble remembering things, we can help them with this; if they are lonely, we can visit them and talk and play with them.)

5. *Will you get old someday?* (Yes.)

   When you get old, will you still be pretty much the same person you were when you were young? (Yes.)

   How can this be? (Answers will be similar to those to Question #1.)

Follow-Up Activities:

ACTIVITY #1

▸ This activity will give the children an opportunity to spend time with an elderly person and help them learn that the critical decision to spend time with the elderly is a good decision to make.

▸ Materials needed: *Interview Sheet* (page 248) for each child.

▸ Reproduce the *Interview Sheet* for each child. Distribute the activity sheet and discuss it with the children. Ask the children to interview someone who is older, like a grandparent. Tell the children the date the completed sheets must be returned. At that time, have the children share their interview results with the group.

▸ Another option is to have the leader invite an older person to come to the class and have the children ask the questions on the activity sheet during class.

ACTIVITY #2

▸ This activity will give the children a chance to spend more time with elderly people and discover the joy it brings to all when this critical decision is made.

▸ Materials needed: Art paper and crayons or markers for each child.

▸ Distribute the paper and crayons or markers to the children and have them draw several cheerful pictures and practice a happy song or two. Then visit a rest home and have the children sing the songs and give their pictures to the residents of the rest home.

  CRITICAL DECISIONS © 2006 MAR✶CO PRODUCTS, INC. 1-800-448-2197

▶ Later, you could have the children write letters or draw more pictures for the residents of the rest home, assigning each a "pen pal." If you decide to do this, you will need to set aside time once a week for the children to write to or draw for their "pen pal."

ACTIVITY #3

▶ This activity will help the children understand that we all grow older.

▶ Materials needed: Baby picture and recent picture of each child; art paper, pencils, and crayons for each child; bulletin board

▶ Have the children bring in a baby picture and a recent picture of themselves. Distribute two pieces of art paper about the same size as the pictures, a pencil, and crayons to each child.

▶ Have the children write their names at the top of the two blank picture-sized pieces of art paper. Then instruct them to draw on one piece of paper a picture that shows what they believe they will look like when they are grown. On the other piece of paper, instruct them to draw a picture of what they believe they will look like when they are old.

▶ When everyone has finished, have the children share their pictures with the class.

▶ Discuss how they will still be the same person no matter what age they become.

▶ Put the children's photographs and pictures on a bulletin board and title it: *No Matter What Age I Am, I Am Still An Important And Special Person.*

(Note: Remind the children that making the critical decision to spend time with the elderly means spending time only with elderly people they know very well and who are safe or if they are with an adult they know well. Remind them NOT to talk with any elderly person who is a stranger.)

CAPTAIN CALVIN'S MAGIC SNOW DANCE

My name is Joshua Jacob Nell. I am a grown man now, but I am going to tell you a story about me when I was just five years old. It was then that I made the decision to spend time with someone in my family who was elderly, and I sure am glad I did.

My story starts like this …

One day when my dad and mom had vacation, they helped move my grandpa into our house. I really didn't know my grandpa very well until he moved in with us. I remember peeking through the window and seeing Grandpa get out of the van with my dad. They started walking up the sidewalk to our house, and they each had two big suitcases full of Grandpa's things. He looked old and full of wrinkles. He didn't have much hair, either. I was sure I wouldn't like him.

Mom and Dad made me help carry some of Grandpa's things inside. I didn't think this was fair. My sister, Jenna Kate, did not have to help unload anything because she was at a movie with her friends. I told Mom and Dad that I wanted to go to the movies, too, and did not want to help. But they made me help, anyway.

About this time, I thought to myself, "Grandpa is going to be boring." I even thought he was a little scary.

Reader: Pause. Ask the children the following question, then continue reading the story.

Why do you think Joshua thought his grandpa was boring or scary? (Joshua thought this because his grandfather was old. He did not know that older people can be just as much fun as younger people.)

I was really wrong about my grandfather being boring and scary. He was truly a lot of fun to be around. You see, my grandpa taught me lots of fun things while he lived with us. He taught me how to plant corn, how to fish, how to tie my shoelaces, and even how to draw submarines and sharks. He taught me these and many, many more things. But the best thing my grandpa taught me was how to make it snow!

I'm going to tell you all about this, so listen carefully.

After we helped Grandpa move his things into the guest bedroom across the hall from me, I remember him asking me to come into his room. I did not want to do this, but I knew I would get into trouble with my parents if I didn't, so I went on in.

I remember Grandpa thanking me for being such a big help to him. Then he said jokingly, "Joshua Jacob Nell, I'm glad to be across the hall from you. I now consider myself to be your neighbor. Let me introduce myself. I am Calvin Brandon Nell, and I am pleased to know you." Then he stood up very tall and saluted me. I couldn't help but smile. He asked me how old I was and I told him I was five.

Then he said, "Five! Why you are old enough to get your military name, son. Let's see, I am called Captain Calvin by all my friends. Since you are my grandson, there's no reason why you couldn't be a captain, too. I think a good name for you would be Captain JJ. What do you think about that name? Do you like it, son?"

I *loved* that name! I really did, and I told Grandpa I loved it. The name he gave me made me feel big and important. Grandpa then stood tall and saluted me again. This time, I copied him and returned his salute.

I remember, just like it was yesterday, that Captain Calvin then stopped to think. He was very quiet and he rubbed his beard. He asked me, "Captain JJ, since you are already five years old, I bet you already know how to do the Magic Snow Dance. Don't you, son?

"I don't know about a Magic Snow Dance, Captain Calvin," I replied.

Captain Calvin smiled at me and said, "Well, bless my whiskers! (I loved it when he said this.) I am certainly glad I moved next door, because it is high time you learned it. All captains need to know how to do the Magic Snow Dance."

Now he had ALL my attention! He told me that he had been reading the newspaper in the van while Dad drove him to our house. He said he noticed in the weather section some days when it was cold enough to snow. I remember he said to me, "Captain JJ, after looking at the weather page, I think this Tuesday would be a good day for me to teach you the Magic Snow Dance."

"Really?" I asked excitedly.

"Yes," Captain Calvin replied. "Tuesday would be a perfect day. I read in the paper there was a chance of snow on that day, but if we did our Magic Snow Dance REALLY WELL … I think we could encourage that snow to come on down for sure. Do you want to give it a try?"

I remember shouting, "Yes, sir! I *do* want to give it a try." In fact, I told Captain Calvin, "I want to try it right now!" After all, this was Saturday. Tuesday was three long days away.

"I'm sorry, Captain JJ," he said to me. "We will need to wait until Tuesday to do the dance. I still have a lot of unpacking to do and I am really tired from the long drive here. We will just have to wait until Tuesday." Then I remember him informing me, "I have a feeling that if we wait until Tuesday, our Magic Snow Dance will really work."

"OK," I said. "I guess I can wait."

That night, while in bed waiting to go to sleep, I wondered if the Magic Snow Dance really *would* work.

I remember waiting for what seemed to be forever. But Tuesday finally came! Captain Calvin's eyes smiled as he said, "This is the day, Captain JJ. I have a feeling that this is the day we can dance that snow right on down."

I remember Captain Calvin bending down and looking straight into my eyes. He said, "OK, Captain JJ, what you have to do to learn the Magic Snow Dance is to follow me, and do what I do." Captain Calvin led me into our living room. He stood across from the TV, right on the edge of our round braided rug.

He raised his left arm. I raised mine.

Then he raised his right arm. I raised mine.

He took one step forward, then another. I did, too.

Faster now and with arms and legs in a flurry, we danced around and around the braided rug.

Dizzy with delight, we did the Magic Snow Dance. Grandpa would laugh and I would, too.

After the Magic Snow Dance, we flopped down together on the couch. Then we giggled until our eyes got watery and tears rolled down our cheeks.

Captain Calvin finally got his breath and said, "Captain JJ, I am glad we are becoming friends."

Reader: Pause. Ask the children the following questions, then continue reading the story.

Do you think Joshua is glad he has made the critical decision to spend time with his grandfather? (Yes.)

How can you tell? (They are doing fun things together and laughing with each other. Joshua knows he would have missed out on having a wonderful friend if he hadn't decided to spend time with his grandfather.)

"We are becoming BEST friends!" I agreed.

Later, that evening, when Mom tucked me into bed, I lay there in the darkness waiting for morning. Hoping … wondering … believing.

Then morning came. The sun was making its entrance as I rubbed my sleepy eyes and stretched a long, tingly, good-morning stretch.

Remembering the snow dance, I anxiously yet cautiously faced the curtains of my bedroom window. With the bravest of thoughts, I whispered, "I believe. I believe." Then I pushed back the drapes.

SNOW!

The yard looked like a huge birthday cake with thick vanilla icing.

"It worked," I yelled. "It worked! We helped the snow come down."

I scrambled over the bed and raced across the hall to Captain Calvin's room. I climbed up the side of his bed and shook his shoulders. "We did it, Captain Calvin! Our Magic Snow Dance worked!" The captain's sleepy eyes twinkled when they opened and his whole face smiled a special, happy smile.

I remember thinking to myself as I hugged Captain Calvin tightly, "I'm glad I decided to get to know and spend time with my grandpa."

And even though I am grown now, I will always continue to be glad I made that critical decision to spend time with my grandfather. Captain Calvin will always hold a bright spot in my memory.

INTERVIEW SHEET

My name is _____

I interviewed _____

1.   What are some things that we use now that had not been invented when you were growing up?

   _____

   _____

2.   What was school like when you were growing up and going to school?

   _____

   _____

3.   Are there any things that you think were better when you were growing up than they are now?

   _____

   _____

4.   What clothes were popular for girls to wear?

   _____

   _____

5.   What clothes were popular for boys to wear?

   _____

   _____

6.   What did kids do for fun when you were growing up?

   _____

   _____

7.   What advice do you have for kids who are growing up in this time?

   _____

   _____

8.   Do you have a memory of some fun times growing up that you would like to share with me?

   _____

   _____

9.   What kind of music did you like to listen to when you were growing up?

   _____

10.   Do you remember any dances that were popular when you were growing up?

   _____